Real Estate Auctions:
An Investment Guide
For Buyers

Jack Pantleo

Dedication

This book is dedicated to Dianna, Laura, Tracy, Krumbutton, and especially to Ed.

I want to thank my father-in-law, Ed, for his help in showing me how to select and acquire investment property. Before I became a real estate broker, I had always wanted to invest in real estate. Ed had over twenty years of real estate experience and he understood market cycles. He knew how to select properties that would not only yield positive cash flows as rentals but would also have good potential for future appreciation.

One of the first things Ed told me regarding real estate investing is that "many people want to invest in real estate, but they just don't know how." My goal in writing this book is to "show people how" by sharing my experiences and recommendations.

Table of Contents:

Introduction

Recently, I attended a real estate auction in search of a property to purchase as a rental. While waiting for the auctioneer to arrive, I had a conversation with a man standing next to me who wanted to purchase an investment property. During our conversation I mentioned that I was a real estate broker and that I had been investing in real estate for several years. I told him about my recent experiences helping two family members purchase investment/ rental properties at auction. He started to ask me questions--lots of questions. This was his first real estate auction so he had several questions about the auction process itself and some general questions concerning real estate investing and the rental market. His questions were all insightful. I could tell he had a background in business and that he was careful when it came to investing.

After a while he confided to me that he was interested in purchasing the property in which we were standing. I told him I was hoping to purchase the three bedroom, two bath condo listed at the bottom of the flyer provided to us at the auction site. (This particular auction was different from others I had attended in that it took place on the lawn of one of the properties to be auctioned off. There were only 35 properties to be auctioned that day and instead of renting a large meeting room at an area hotel, the auction company divided the properties into smaller groups of five to six homes located in close proximity. One property from each group was then selected by the auction company as the location to hold the auction for the other properties within the group.)

The auctioneer finally arrived and all of us who had been waiting filled out the registration forms and took our places on the front lawn. The auctioneer reviewed the bidding process, explained that the purpose of the auction was to collect the highest bids for their clients and then informed the crowd that it would be at the discretion of their clients as to whether or not the offers would be accepted. He went on to say that the high bidders would be notified within seven days if their bid had been accepted and if they could therefore proceed with the actual purchase of the property. The auction started with excitement and within twenty minutes all properties within this group were auctioned. The highest bidders were selected.

The man I spoke to earlier came up to me with a disappointed look on his face. He did not get the property he wanted. He also asked me one more question: **"Hey, you didn't even bid on the property you wanted! Why?"** Of all the questions he asked, this one was the most difficult to answer. I spent the next few minutes with him sitting on the front steps of his home "that was not to be." I showed him the information I had collected about the property and I shared with him some of my thoughts and philosophy about real estate investing. He seemed to appreciate what I told him.

As a result of that discussion, and similar discussions with past clients, I decided to write this book. In the pages that follow, I will make recommendations on: 1) selecting real estate to purchase at auction (as either a residence or investment property), 2) determining what the property is worth, 3) deciding how much to bid, 4) how to bid, and 5) determining how many properties to acquire.

The reader will notice that the book includes chapters on: 1) preparing a property to be a rental, 2) finding and selecting a renter, and 3) deciding when it is time to sell the property. In order to make a profitable real estate investment, investors must consider the complete cycle of investing from acquiring a property to selling it. When the real estate market is "down" (i.e., real estate values have declined and continue to decline) investors can not just acquire a property in need of repairs, make those repairs, sell the property, and realize a profit. A "middle part" needs to be included in the investment cycle. In a "down" market, the middle part corresponds to the renting and maintenance of the property that allows the investor to hold the property until it is time to sell. In other words, the investor needs to hold the property until the value of real estate increases to a level that will result in a profit for the investor. Failure to understand the costs and effort involved with holding real estate for a prolonged and/or unknown period of time will lead to a failure to make a profit.

It is my hope that the guidelines provided in this book will assist investors in buying property at auction, and in addition to helping buy at auction, these guidelines will also help investors make profitable decisions on real estate obtained by other means including inheritance, foreclosure sales, private party purchases, etc.

Chapter 1: Three Primary Types of Real Estate Auctions

Real estate auctions are activities whereby the seller, usually a mortgage company, hires an auction company to dispose of real estate via a bidding process. It is the job of the auction company to advertise the auction in order to attract potential buyers (i.e., bidders) and to coordinate a process whereby potential buyers compete for the purchase of a property. A brief overview of three primary types of real estate auctions will be provided in this chapter. The three types are: Live Auctions, Sealed-bid Auctions, and Internet Auctions.

Live Auctions

As the name implies, live real estate auctions correspond to an activity whereby potential bidders actively compete against one another to purchase a property. Auctioneers (and auctioneer assistants) are used to coordinate the bidding and select the highest bidder.

The process is quite similar to traditional farm or livestock auctions. The auctioneer starts the bidding at a pre-determined level and then "works" the crowd to solicit bids. The auctioneer's rhythmic "chant" helps create excitement and interest in the bidding process. The auctioneer and the assistants (sometimes called bidding assistants) keep track of who made the last bid and the amount of that bid. Previous bidders are then prodded to bid higher. The process is exciting, fast-paced, and very loud.

It is important that people buying property at auction not get "caught up" in the excitement. I have seen occasions where people pay more for a property at auction than what they would have paid if they had purchased the same property just a few weeks earlier by the regular method of submitting an offer to the owner (i.e., mortgage company.) Do your homework; have a pre-determined maximum bid amount for every property you are considering bidding on.

Also, it is important to note that auction companies will "allow" you to bid against yourself. If you have a question about who bid last and the amount of that bid, be sure to ask one of the auction assistants for assistance. In Chapter 6, Auction Day, I provide more information on how to prepare for the live auction, what to bring with you to the auction, and the auction process itself.

Sealed-bid Auctions

Sealed-bid auctions are often used by Government agencies to dispose of properties. Registration is required before a sealed bid can be submitted. Potential buyers submit a bid in writing for a specific property to a contact provided at a predefined location. Bids are accepted for a specified length of time (possibly from just a few hours to several days) and then the highest bidder is identified. The winning bid amount and the name of the individual making that bid is announced publicly. Individuals who submitted bids on the property, but who were not selected at the highest bidder, are usually allowed to view a list of all bids submitted in order to determine how their bid compared with the others.

Internet Auctions

Internet auctions are becoming more prevalent. They are less expensive to operate than traditional auctions and more convenient for many of the potential bidders. Usually, internet auctions are used for lower-value property like older homes located in remote areas or bare land. For example, assume an auction property is located in a remote part of state. It would be costly to have an auction company send people to that site to dispose of just one property. If the property was auctioned during a larger auction held in a metropolitan area located some distance away from the property, this might discourage some local people from participating in the auction. (People living in the same remote area as the auction property might be the best potential buyers.) In this situation, an internet auction will probably yield the best results for the seller.

Internet auctions can be either a sealed-bid or live auction format. Internet auctions will also require potential bidders to register is advance and earnest money is collected via credit card. Some internet auctions will accept bids for a pre-determined period of time and then notify the highest bidder that they had won. Other auctions are based on achieving a pre-determined amount for the property. Once that amount is obtained, the auction process stops and the individual submitting the bid is notified that they are the successful bidder.

Software is now available that allows potential bidders to log onto an auction company's web site and participate in a live auction being conducted by the auction company on auction day. It is less noisy than being at the actual auction site and is more convenient for some buyers since they do not have to travel. This on-line form of internet auction also has the advantage of immediately letting the bidder know that they have submitted the highest bid. The highest bidder is either instructed to proceed to a designated area to sign a purchase contract or forms are emailed to the high bidder for their signature. Hard copies of the signed e-mailed forms (i.e., purchase agreement, etc.) are then mailed back to the auction company.

Preliminary Words of Encouragement and Caution

There are a two things I want to emphasize to my readers early in this book. First, auctions can be a great place to buy real estate--but don't expect to get a $100,000 property for $1,000. Buyers must be realistic with regard to the amount they will need to bid. With a little luck, however, you might be able to obtain a property for 40% to 60% of what it sold for during the last peak of real estate prices. Second, if you are considering buying real estate at auction you must do your "homework." Remember, you are buying the property "As Is." How much is the property worth? How much should you bid? What will the repairs cost? If the property is being purchased as a rental, what will it rent for? What will the property sell for in the future? How long will you need to hold the property before you can sell it for a profit? My intent for the chapters that follow is to provide answers to questions like the ones above.

Chapter 2: How to Select a Property to Use as a Personal Residence

All real estate is an investment. However, when a property is purchased as a residence and not with the intent of providing income, different priorities and requirements exist relating to the selection of that property.

NOTE: I will use the terms Real Estate Agent, Agent, Real Estate Broker, and Realtor interchangeably throughout this book.

Step Number 1: Get Started on Your Financing

The first question all potential home buyers should ask themselves is "How much can we afford?" Auction companies will occasionally publish starting bids on their inventory list. An inventory list is a printed listing or brochure of properties that are to be auctioned. The inventory list usually includes: 1) the address of the property, 2) general information concerning size of the home in square feet, number of bedrooms and bathrooms and 3) a starting or minimum bid amount for the property. Sometimes the starting bids are as low as $1,000. Do not decide to bid on a property based on the published starting bids. These starting bids do nothing more than help to create excitement within potential bidders. We would all like to purchase a $100,000 property for $1,000. It will not happen. However, if potential buyers know in advance how much they can afford and use that information (combined with information on what the home is worth) to determine a reasonable upper limit to their bidding, they just might get a real bargain!

Do not miss out on a potential great deal because you decide to use an unrealistically low amount for a maximum bid. These properties will not last forever--there might not be other opportunities for you to acquire property at such a discounted price.

Talk to your bank and other lenders recommended by family, friends, or your real estate agent, to determine the loan amount you can "qualify" for (i.e., the maximum amount of money the lenders are willing to loan you). Next, have the potential lenders provide you with Good Faith Estimates (GFE's) for that maximum amount. I recommend you check with at least three different lenders. Review the GFE's for fees and interest rates, pay particular attention to the APR.

***Annual Percentage Rate (APR)** is a method used to disclose the "cost" of borrowing money in a standardized way. In other words, the APR is the total cost of credit to the consumer, expressed as an annual percentage of the amount of credit granted. It is intended to make it easier to compare lenders and loan options. The APR is likely to differ from the advertised "note rate" or "headline rate" because of the addition of associated one-time fees charged by the lender.*

If you have questions regarding the loan application fees or the proposed interest rate, ask the lenders to explain. If you prefer to do business with one of the lenders over the others, but their APR is higher than the competitors, feel free to submit the other GFE's to the lender you prefer and ask them to meet or beat the competing offers.

Once you have selected a potential lender, ask them to provide you with a pre-approval letter. Do not pay any application fees or other charges at this time. The GFE's and pre-approval letters are services that potential lenders should offer you free of charge. Final loan application and approval will occur after you have a purchase contract in place. Loan application fees and the cost of the appraisal will be included in the closing costs associated with the final settlement and will be paid (by you, the buyer) at closing.

> *Be Truthful With Your Lender. It is important to be truthful when applying for a loan and to include any and all negative or positive information regarding your credit, income, assets, and encumbrances to potential lenders. Attempting to hide credit problems or judgments against you, will either slow down the loan approval process or possibly result in a failure to get a loan. Either of these problems could result in a loss of the property and a loss of your earnest money.*

This is also the time to inform the lender of your intent to purchase a residence either at auction, as a short-sale, or as a foreclosure. It is necessary that you inform the lender before purchasing a "distressed" property because the processes involved with an auction property or property obtained from similar transactions, often require more time to complete.

> A **Short-Sale** is a situation whereby a property is being offered for sale by the owner for an amount that is less than what the owner actually owes on the property. In order for this transaction to be completed, the mortgagee (i.e., the one that holds the lien on the property) must be willing to accept less money than is owed by the mortgagor (i.e., the one who pledges property as security for a loan.
>
> There are two reasons for a mortgagee to accept a short-sale condition. The first is declining real estate values. If real estate values are in a decline, the longer the time it takes to sell the property, the less the property might be worth in the future. Since the foreclosure process takes time, it might be in the best interest of the mortgagee to "get rid" of the property as soon as possible. The second reason has to do with the cost of foreclosing on a property. Foreclosing requires legal services, property management services, real estate sales fees, etc. All of this costs money. Combine the effects of declining real estate values with the costs associated with foreclosing on a property, and it is obvious why lenders are willing to do short-sales.
>
> **Foreclosure** corresponds to the termination of all rights of a mortgagor to the property covered by a mortgage. If the mortgagor misses payments on

the property, the mortgage holder (mortgagee) will use legal means to acquire the property that was held as security for a loan. This property will then be sold (disposed of) by the mortgagee to pay the loan.

Distressed Property corresponds to a property that is either going through foreclosure or impending foreclosure.

Even though a purchase contract may require the buyer to complete the sale within 30 days, the sellers often have the ability, and the need, to "string out" the actual closing for as long as two to three extra months in order to clear various problems including title issues. As a buyer, you will need a lender that is willing to commit to funding a loan with potentially extended closing dates.

Interest Rate Locks. When buyers are approved for a loan, the lender will provide them with a "lock" on the interest rate they will charge for the loan. Be aware that a lock on an interest rate is usually good for only 30 to 45 days. If the closing to purchase the property goes past the "lock" period for the interest rate, be prepared for a rate change. It has been my experience that when interest rates change (in situations like these) the interest rates go up, not down!

As an example, two of my buyers recently closed on auction properties. Both buyers were informed by the auction company that they needed to be able to close within 30 days. After 30 days, however, the title company was still not ready to set closing dates for the properties. I was told by their customer representative that the title company was waiting for final approval from the sellers (i.e., mortgage company).

After two more weeks passed, I was finally able to set a closing time and date for one of the properties. My client and I arrived at the title company for the closing and we were informed that the closing would need to be delayed because the seller was still negotiating a pay-off with the Homeowner's Association. I immediately informed the title company office manager that my client had taken off from work for the closing and it would be difficult to re-schedule. As the buyer's broker (and a potential source of future business for the title company) I asked the office manager to contact the seller and inform them of the problem. She agreed to contact the seller personally. Within a few hours, the negotiations between the seller and the HOA were settled and the closing was completed.

The second property was not granted final sale approval by the seller until the following week and closed shortly thereafter. During my conversations with the manager of the title company, I was informed that they had been "slammed" with over 200 closings resulting from the same auction. The first properties to close were the "cash" deals. They closed first because they were "easy." (Both of my buyers were cash buyers.) The next properties to close were the ones requiring financing that had buyers who were represented by an agent. (Title companies will prioritize their closings based on potential future business. Since referrals from real estate agents are the foundation of their business, transactions involving agents will get priority.) The last properties to close were the ones requiring financing with buyers who did not have agents.

Step Number 2: Select Potential Properties From the Auction Schedule

Determine your requirements for a home. How many bedrooms and bathrooms do you need? What area do you want to live in? What style of home do you want? Make a list of your requirements--include the things you must have and things you would like to have but are not necessary. For example, an over-sized two-car garage is nice, but you would settle for a regular two-car garage. Review the auction schedule published by the auction company and select those homes that meet your requirements. Drive by the homes that seem to have potential and take notes regarding the neighborhood quality and general condition of the exterior.

Visit the homes during the scheduled open houses or arrange for a private showing with the listing agent or if you have an agent, have your agent set a showing. Bring your digital camera, take lots of pictures and take notes (or complete a home buyer checklist like the one provided at the end of this chapter.) Pay particular attention to the items that need to be repaired. Will a homeowner need to repair the items prior to moving in or can the items wait to be repaired? What will the repairs cost? This information will be needed for the comparison of properties and in determining how much to bid or even if a bid on a particular property should be considered.

I recommend potential buyers introduce themselves to some of the neighbors and ask them about the schools, the neighborhood, and the home itself. If a potential buyer is not familiar with the area, it is also a good idea for them to drive around the neighborhood checking for parks, busy streets, nature trails, school locations, shopping, etc. Look for the "good" and the "bad." Un-kept yards, noisy dogs, junk cars, and neighboring homes in poor condition will affect your property values and your quality of life. **This can not be overstated--where you live has a big impact on the quality of your life.**

Step Number 3: Determine a "Comp Value" for Each Property of Interest

Once potential buyers have selected one or more properties of interest, they should meet with their Realtor and examine **"Sold Comps"** (up to the past 18 months) and **"Active Comps"** from the subdivisions where the properties are located. When comparing the properties of interest to the "Comps," allowances will need to be made for the differences between them (i.e., three bedrooms versus two,1,400 finished square feet versus 1,200, one-car garage versus a two-car garage, etc.) Your agent will be able to place a dollar amount on these differences so that a comparison is possible. Use the "Comps" to determine a **"Comp Value"** for each property.

"Comps" or "Comparables" correspond to properties, similar to the subject property, that are used as "references" to help determine an estimate of value for the subject property. "Comps" can refer to homes that have sold, "Sold Comps," or to homes currently on the market, "Active Comps." "Sold Comps" corresponding to homes that have recently sold are usually a better indication of a home's market value than "Active Comps." However, when real estate values are changing rapidly, either up or down, it is important to reference both the "Sold" and "Active Comparables."

A *"Comp Value"* for a subject property is an estimate of value resulting from the comparison of properties after adjustments are made for the differences between them. For example, if the comparable properties are not identical, adjustments (i.e., approximate values assigned to the differences) will need to be made to each reference property to compensate for differences in size, condition, date of sale, location, number of bedrooms, bathrooms, garage size, etc., so that an adjusted value for each comparable is determined.

A set of adjusted values results and the range of those values is used to express the *"Comp Value"* for the subject property (i.e., the value of the subject property falls between $245,000 and $260,000). (Sometimes, a single value within that range, corresponding to a property that most closely resembles the subject property, is selected to express the value of the subject property.)

The process of determining a home's "Comp Value" is also referred to as the *"Sales Comparison Approach"* or the *"Market Data Approach"* to finding the value of a property. Information needed to determine "Comp Values" can be obtained by your Realtor from the Realtor's Multiple Listing Service (MLS). See definition below.

<u>Home buyers should ask their agent to show them some of the homes corresponding to the "Active Comps" information they viewed</u>. This is necessary in order to get a good understanding of the differences that exist between homes available through regular methods, like homes offered for sale by a homeowner (through a Realtor) and the auction properties. Homebuyers should keep in mind that it is easier to purchase a home through the traditional method of submitting an offer and having that offer either accepted, countered, or rejected by a homeowner than buying a home at auction. The traditional method is also less risky in most states because it will allow the buyer time to hire a professional home inspector and negotiate repairs (or cancel the purchase contract) if problems are found with the home after the purchase agreement is made. With an auction property, the property is purchased "As Is."

The **Multiple Listing Service (MLS)** is a database system developed and maintained by Realtors to share information with fellow Realtors on properties currently on the market and sales information on properties that have sold in the past. Information stored in the database includes: size of home, number of bedrooms, number of baths, garage size, seller concessions, list price, selling price, days on market, etc.

Information on homes currently on the market is often being made public in many parts of the United States through IDX (Information Data Exchange) services to web sites like Realtor.com. However, information on homes that have sold is rarely available to the general public, it is usually made available only to Realtors who are members of the MLS. In order for private citizens to obtain "sold information" they will need to either contact a Realtor who is a member of the MLS or contact the county in which the property resides for **Public Record Information** maintained by that county.

Some counties within the United States are now making this data available over the Internet. However, the information maintained by the county will usually include only the price a home sold for and the date it sold. Other important sales information including days on market, sales concessions, and condition of the property is not included. Check with your local county government to see what Public Record Information is available in your area.

Step Number 4: Review the Disclosures

Auction companies often provide Disclosures with the properties they will be auctioning. The Disclosures document known problems with the properties. Disclosures can usually be found on the auction company's web site. Some auction companies will notify potential bidders of problems with the property on auction day by handing out hard copies of the Disclosures before the bidding starts. Sometimes they have the auctioneer say something like "you should not bid on this property unless you know what you are doing" just before they start accepting bids on the property in question. I have even seen properties come back on auction within minutes of being "sold" because the high bidder was notified of defects just prior to filing out the Purchase Agreement.

Step Number 5: Hire a Professional Home Inspector

Once you have found a home you would like to bid on, it might be necessary to have the home examined by a professional home inspector and/or a structural engineer. If, during the review of the Disclosures (or during a visit to the property) a problem is found that is of concern, I recommend that professional advice be obtained. It is not uncommon for homes being sold at auction to have problems. Perhaps the problems are serious enough that a buyer decides against bidding on the property. If the buyer does decide to bid on the property, the inspection information can be used to obtain an estimate of the cost of the repairs. This would help determine how much to bid. Large cracks in walls, floors that slope, stains on the ceiling, and doors that will not shut properly are just some of the indications that problems, possibly serious ones, might exist.

As an investor, I tend to shy away from homes that appear to have major problems or structural issues. Occasionally, homes do appear at auction that are potentially great deals if the buyer has the funds needed to hire the expertise to evaluate the condition of the home and make any necessary repairs. Early this summer there was a $1,000,000 plus home being auctioned in my area with a starting bid of $600,000. The home was built on a cliff with the back of the home resting on stilts. It seems the ground underneath the home was unstable and the home was starting to slide down the drop-off. The home did sell and the person who bought it for $650,000 must have been convinced the problem could be resolved. This is not anything I would do or recommend.

Step Number 6: Determine a Discount Factor

There is one item in particular that I recommend potential buyers of homes at auction should consider. That item is a "discount amount" to be factored into a potential high bid. Most people attend a real estate auction with the intent of obtaining a property at a bargain price.

This is not always the case. Moreover, buying property at auction does have disadvantages with regard to potential delays in closing and risks due to the fact the property is being purchased "As Is." With this in mind, I recommend potential buyers of auction properties also factor in a reduction or discount factor to compensate for these disadvantages and risks.

During the auctions I attend, I record the final sales price of all the properties sold. At a later time, I identify properties from the auction list that are similar to the ones that my clients would like to purchase. I then compare the auction sale prices of the similar properties to the final sales prices of comparable properties in the MLS and note the difference. During two recent auctions, I noticed a difference of about 20%. In other words, properties at these two auctions had a tendency to sell for about 20% less than what comparable properties sold for through the MLS. I use this amount as a "discount factor" or guide in determining the maximum amount to bid on properties at future auctions.

Step Number 7: Determine a Preliminary Maximum Bid Amount for Each Property

Start with the "Comp Value." Modify the "Comp Value" by subtracting the "Discount Factor" to determine a Preliminary Maximum Bid Amount for the properties. For example, a property with a "Comp Value" of $100,000 would have a $80,000 Preliminary Maximum Bid Amount after a 20% discount factor is applied.

Step Number 8: Consider the "Other" Important Factors and Determine a Final Maximum Bid Amount for Each Property

Notice that I referred to the value determined during Step Number 7 as the **Preliminary Maximum Bid Amount**. "Comp Values" incorporate many of the objective or quantifiable factors involved in determining the value of property. There are, however, other factors (sometimes subjective or "personal") that need to be considered when deciding how much to bid on a home.

Perhaps a buyer believes a particular property has more "investment potential" than other properties. For example, suppose there are two homes that are nearly identical. The only thing they differ on is the size of the garage. One home has a one-car garage and the other a two-car. The "Comp Values" for these properties were adjusted to factor in the value of the different garage sizes. The adjustment was based on sales history. However, the buyer believes that in the future, homes with two-car garages will increase in value more (and at a faster rate) than homes with just a one-car garage. (This buyer might decide to increase the "Maximum Bid Amount" for the property with the two-car garage.)

An example of a "personal" factor could be the location of the home. Assume the buyers have found a home they like that is located close to their place of employment. Is a ten minute commute to work versus a forty-five minute commute worth an extra $10,000 (or $60.00 per month increase in a mortgage payment)? It would be if the price of gas rises to what it was during 2008. (These buyers might decide to increase the "Preliminary Maximum Bid Amount" for the property located closer to their place of employment.)

In summary, it is important to mention that sometimes it is "OK" to pay more for a home than what an "objective evaluation" might support. There is nothing wrong with that as long as the buyers are aware of how much they are paying extra and why they are willing to pay the extra amount.

Questions:

1) Is it worth increasing the "Preliminary Maximum Bid Amount" to get a home your family really wants? (I think it is!)

2) How much is it worth to have a home located at the end of a cul-de-sac when you have young children learning to ride bicycles?

3) What is the value of a large backyard with a high fence that backs to open space when you own two large dogs?

As an example of determining how much to bid at an auction, consider the following:

Auction Property A

Features: 3 Bedrooms, 2 Bathrooms, 1,250 finished squared feet, unfinished basement, attached 2-car garage.

Repairs needed: new furnace, new water heater, new carpet, new vinyl flooring in kitchen and both baths, grass needs to be planted in both front and back yards.

Estimated Cost of Repairs: $8,200

Estimated Value From "Sold Comps:" $165,000

Other Considerations: This property is in average condition for the neighborhood. The buyers prefer a home with four bedrooms, however, the oldest son would be leaving for college soon and a bedroom area in the basement could suffice. The home has an attached 2-car garage but the buyers only have one car and do not need the extra garage space. Their Realtor has encouraged them to acquire this home because he believes the two-car garage will have more "investment potential" (i.e., make the buyers more money in the future). Previous auction properties from this neighborhood sold for about 15% less than comparable sales reported by the MLS. Due to the investment potential corresponding to the two-car garage, the buyers have decided to use only a 10% discount factor instead of 15%. The Maximum Bid Amount determined for this property is $165,000 - 10% discount factor = $148,500.

Maximum Bid Amount Determined for This Property: $148,500

Auction Property B

Features: 4 Bedrooms, 2 Bathrooms, 1,250 finished squared feet, unfinished basement, no garage.

Repairs needed: new furnace, new water heater, new carpet, new vinyl flooring in kitchen and both baths

Estimated Cost of Repairs: $6,200

Estimated Value From "Sold Comps:" $155,000

Other Considerations: This property is also in average condition for the neighborhood and does have four bedrooms. This home did have an attached 1-car garage at one time but the previous owners converted the garage space to an extra bedroom. Their Realtor informed them that converting the 1-car garage to an extra bedroom did not increase the value of the home (and might have actually decreased the value). This home is in the same neighborhood as Property B. Prior auction sales for this neighborhood seem to sell for about 15% less than comparable sales reported in the MLS and as a result, the buyers have decided to factor in a full 15% reduction for their maximum bid ($155,000 - 15% = $131,750).

Maximum Bid Amount Determined for This Property: $131,750

Auction Property C

Features: 4 Bedrooms, 2 Bathrooms, 1,350 finished squared feet, unfinished basement, 1-car attached garage.

Repairs needed: new furnace, new water heater, new kitchen and bathroom cabinets, new roof, new carpet, new vinyl flooring in kitchen and both baths

Estimated Cost of Repairs: $16,700

Estimated Value From "Sold Comps:" $145,000

Other Considerations: This property is in below average condition for the neighborhood in which it resides but does have four bedrooms and an attached 1-car garage. This home is in a different neighborhood than Properties A & B. Prior auction sales for this neighborhood sell for about 15% less than comparable sales reported by the MLS. This home does need new cabinets and a new roof. Due to the amount of "out of pocket money" required to make repairs, the buyers have decided not to bid on this property.

Maximum Bid Amount Determined for This Property: N/A

With regard to the above properties, the buyers decided to bid on property A an B only. The loan package they selected requires 5% down at closing. The buyers do have $19,000 in cash available for closing costs and repairs but the amount of cash needed for Property C would take too much of their cash even if it were obtained at a very low purchase price.

The above exercise was not intended to be a precise dollar per item adjustment for all relevant factors. What was intended was an example of what buyers must go through to determine if a property should be bid on and how much to bid. It is important that buyers: 1) document the differences between the properties, 2) consider the costs of needed repairs, 3) get advice from their Realtor and other professionals, 4) include their personal preferences for a property, and 5) possibly re-evaluate their original "requirements" for a home.

> *Potential home buyers will be going to an auction not knowing the order in which the properties will be auctioned or the final selling prices of the properties. To improve their chances of obtaining a property, buyers should, if possible, have more than one property identified with a corresponding maximum bid for each. The goal is to obtain a home that "fits" their needs, wants and financial limitations, for an amount that is less than (hopefully much less than) what they would pay for a home listed in the MLS.*

Buyers should keep in mind that the purpose of the Maximum Bid Amount is to provide a guideline during the bidding process. With a little luck, a buyer will acquire the property for less than the Maximum Bid Amount they predetermined. If this happens, the buyer will be able to say that he/she got a "great deal" at the auction.

> **Important:** *Many auction companies add a **5% Buyers Premium** to the final bid to cover costs associated with selling the property (i.e., paying the auction company, the buyer's agent, etc.) In other words, the total amount a buyer pays for the property will be the final bid plus a buyer's premium.*

Case Study #1: Rains, Trains, and Traffic

> *About five years ago I was working with a husband and wife to find them a home. The husband's business had done quite well and they were looking to "move up." We viewed dozens of homes and one day we found one that "knocked their socks off." Some independent builders had joined together and bought a small amount of land just large enough to build about twenty homes. All of the homes were custom, high-end homes with no two being alike. The part that really impressed me was that the builders had left many of the hundred-year-old trees in place and situated the homes so that picture windows sided to the trees instead of neighboring homes.*
>
> *My clients and their children walked through the front door and immediately fell in love with the home. The only thing they could say was "Wow." The family walked into the kitchen and they were stunned. The kitchen looked like it came out of a magazine and was situated so that the sink was in the back corner of the home. There was a window above the sink that looked out onto a huge pine tree that was at least forty feet tall. Next to the tree was a rock pathway that ran up the hill to the rear of the property. As the family*

stepped out of the kitchen onto the back patio there was even more excitement. The backyard was huge. During our previous viewings of homes, the children had asked their parents about getting their own pool and each time the parents responded "the backyard isn't big enough." This time the parents started talking about a pool and where they could put it.

The family explored the home for the next hour. The children selected their bedrooms and soon the topic of conversation was focused on writing an offer. I contacted the listing agent and informed him that we had interest in the home. I asked if there were any offers coming in on the home and he said there were not. He offered to contact me if there was a change in status.

As we left the home I told my clients that I would do a market analysis on the property and prepare a written offer ready for them to insert a price and signatures. We also decided to meet at 9:00am the next morning to view the house one more time and to study the "comps."

When I got back to my office I pulled both the sold "comps" and active "comps" for this subdivision. The "comps" revealed that only two properties had sold in this development over the last 18 months. There were currently ten homes listed for sale in the Multiple Listing Service (MLS) and they had been on the market between three to twenty months. The home my clients were interested in had been on the market for nine months. The list price for all the homes seemed reasonable. The market was "hot." Why haven't these homes sold?

The next morning I arrived at the home early so I could do some investigating before my clients got there. I soon realized why the homes were not selling. The only road to provide access to the entry of the community was a very busy street to the east. I had looked at the home during the middle of the day and the traffic did not seem bad. It was now rush hour and the traffic was backed up for blocks.

When I finally arrived at the home I parked my car in front of the house and unlocked the front door for my clients. I then walked up the hill to explore the area behind the home. The rock path we saw by the pine tree yesterday was not a path. It was actually part of a large drainage system. It appeared ditches had been dug farther up the hill to re-route runoff from rainstorms. At the top of the hill was another surprise; there was a large irrigation canal. The canal was not lined with concrete and seemed fairly fragile. I am not an engineer, but I was raised on a farm. I knew that a big rain storm or a family of gofers could easily cause this canal to rupture. As I looked at the system of drainage ditches below the canal, it was obvious that the drainage system was installed to also divert water in case the canal failed. There was evidence of past problems. The canal had a few "patch jobs" and there were signs of washouts.

To the east was a busy street. To the north was an irrigation canal. It was time to explore the south and the west. I decided to go south first. This was the direction the front of the home faced. I knew there were some train tracks nearby but I had not realized they were so close until I walked to the side of the neighbor's home immediately across from the home my clients were interested in. The train track was at an angle to the development and at the entrance to the development, the tracks seemed to be quite a distance away. Inside the development, however, the tracks were much closer.

To the east was a busy street. To the north an irrigation canal. To the south a train track. What was to the west--a toxic landfill? I did check out the west end of the development. I did not see anything out of the ordinary. By this time, however, nothing would have surprised me.

As I walked back to the property the husband drove up. The wife had driven separately since she had to drop the children off at school. I met him in front of his car and we started to talk. Unfortunately, the traffic noise from the street to the east was so loud that we could hardly hear what each of us were saying. I motioned for him to follow me up the hill to the backyard. As we got further up the hill the large trees helped muffle the traffic noise and we could now easily hear one another.

I showed him the system of drainage ditches and the large canal at the top of the hill. He noticed the "patch jobs" on the canal before I had the opportunity to say anything. I pointed out the washouts. We walked down the hill to the back of the home and re-examined the rock-lined drainage system running parallel to the back and both sides of the home. It was obvious to both of us that this system was too shallow to handle a heavy rainstorm or a failure of the irrigation canal.

The neighbor across the street was up and about so I told my client it would be a good idea for him to introduce himself and ask this person about the neighborhood. I also pointed out the train track that ran behind the neighbor's house. As the husband walked across the street to visit with the neighbor, his wife drove up. I met her at her car and she could sense that something was wrong. I asked her to walk up the hill with me and I showed her the drainage ditches and we talked about the traffic.

The husband soon joined us in the backyard and he shared the information he had acquired from the neighbor. The trains run twice during the night and sometimes early Sunday morning. The neighbor said that he loved the neighborhood and that he did not even notice the trains at night. He said that his wife sometimes complained about the noise and vibrations when the trains went by but it did not bother him. He also said that he had been a locomotive engineer for the railroad for 35 years and that he had just retired. (I am not making any of this up!)

My clients and I entered the home and I asked them to come with me to the kitchen to review the "comps." I showed them that the home we were in had been on the market for nine months, that there were currently nine other homes on the market in this development, and that only two of the homes in this development had sold over the past eighteen months. They seemed a little discouraged.

I gave my clients some time alone and they decided to walk through the home one more time. In a few minutes we re-grouped and began to re-hash everything that had just transpired. The wife told me that other people live by train tracks, she thought they could probably get use to it. The husband mentioned he had an engineer friend at work that could design a drainage system for the backyard and even provide an estimate of what it would cost; we could include an allowance for the cost of an enhanced drainage system with the offer for the house. I asked them if they still wanted to write an offer. They were not sure.

I recommended that we not write an offer at this time. I thought it best to think about everything we had discovered. They agreed and the husband said he would contact his engineer friend and see if he could get him to look at the property within the next few days. The husband told me he would call me as soon as his friend inspected the property and let me know what they decided. We left the property--my clients went home and I went back to my office.

As soon as I got to my office, I started looking for other homes. I remembered the husband talked about playing golf with his friends and even though they had not requested that I look for a home located on a golf course, I thought this would be something that might interest them.

Three days went by and my clients did not call. I decided to call them. When I did call, the wife answered the phone and informed me that they had decided against the home with the rain, train, and traffic problems. I told her I understood but had found something else they might like. She told me she would talk to her husband and give me a call back. A few minutes later I received a call from her and we agreed to meet at the new property that evening.

This next home was also very nice. It did not, however, have the "Wow" factor when we first walked in like the previous home. As we walked out the back door the husband noticed that the home was located on a golf course. He turned to his wife and although he did not say the word "Wow" he had the "Wow" look on his face. He had played on this course. He began to tell us about the course and how much he had enjoyed it.

The wife was smiling but she had not been "Wowed." We decided to check out the basement next. The basement was finished. There was a second family room, a craft room, a game room for the children and plenty of storage. My clients had not thought about buying a home with a finished basement but this was a nice bonus. We then decided to go upstairs to check out the bedrooms. The bedrooms were laid-out very nicely and all three had walk-in closets. My clients were happy, but not ready to write an offer. They wanted to sleep on it for a while.

The next afternoon the wife called me and asked if I could set another showing for Saturday. They wanted to look the house over again and take some measurements. My clients, their two children, and I met at the home early Saturday morning. They carefully examined each room, took measurements, and talked about how they would arrange their furniture. We walked outside and everyone checked the backyard in detail.

As the husband walked around the exterior of the home he said "there's a problem here!" He pointed to two golf balls laying at the side of the house. The husband then walked onto the golf course and examined the paths the golf balls would have to take to end up in the backyard. It appeared they would have to land in an area to the north of the golf course and then roll down the hill to get to the yard. No big deal!

The husband continued to explore the golf course and the surrounding area. I soon heard him call my name and motion for me to come. As I got closer to him I could see why he called me. There was a ditch. In fact it was the same irrigation canal that ran behind the other house. This time things were different. The ditch was situated on the south side of a large earthen embankment. It was fairly obvious that if the ditch were to fail it would be the golf course that got flooded and not the backyard of the home they were looking at.

The family checked out the inside of the home again and then we gathered in the kitchen for a quick meeting. They could find nothing wrong with the house; it had everything they wanted and much more. We talked about the previous home and how they were still disappointed that things had not worked out. The wife told me that they were interested in this present home but wanted to think things over. She would call me in a few days.

Monday morning I received a call from the wife. They thought they might be ready to write the offer, so we decided to meet at my office. I showed them the "comps" for similar homes in the neighborhood. This home seemed to be priced about $30,000 less than what other comparable homes on the golf course had sold for during the last 18 months. That was good!

Finally, my clients decided that they wanted the home. We wrote the offer and I submitted it to the listing agent. The sellers accepted the offer that evening. Two weeks later my buyers did their inspection. The professional inspector hired by the buyers could find only minor problems with the home. The problems were submitted to the sellers in an inspection report and the sellers agreed to make all requested repairs. With the exception of the sellers trying to back out of the deal a short time after the inspection, the closing took place about 45 days after the offer was written and accepted. I contacted my clients one month after the closing to see how things were going. They were very happy with their new home and quite relieved they did not buy the home with the rain, train, and traffic problems.

I included the above case study because it provides many examples of the emotions and the problems that buyers do experience while looking for a property to use as a residence. People do form emotional attachments to homes. Unfortunately, buyers are not always able to acquire the home they "really want." When buyers are not able to acquire a home they want, the resulting frustration and disappointment will affect their perception of other homes and their motivation to continue the search. <u>Buyers must be aware of their emotions and must work to make sure their emotions do not interfere with the effort to obtain a home.</u>

<u>Moreover, people must not let an emotional attachment to a home blind them to problems that might exist with the home.</u> The above case study underscores the fact that buying a home at auction requires potential buyers to have all their questions answered and concerns addressed prior to auction day. Remember, there is no negotiation process other than the actual bidding. There is no Inspection Clause. If the potential buyer has the highest bid, they acquire the property "As Is."

Treat Your Home as an Investment

Once a home has been obtained, homeowners should remember that *"all real estate is an investment."* Your home might be the biggest and best investment you ever make. Once you have acquired your property, continue to think of it as an investment. Take care of it by repairing items that need to be repaired and work to increase the value of your home.

Several resources exist that provide information on what a homeowner might expect in terms of return on investment for kitchen remodels, room additions, and other major re-model and renovation projects. Also, talk to your Realtor. He or she will be able to give their professional opinion on the value of renovations, remodels, or additions. For example, adding an over-sized 2-car garage in some neighborhoods may add a significant increase in value whereas converting a 1-car garage to an extra bedroom might actually decrease the value of a home.

A homeowner does not always need to make major renovations--identify small, inexpensive, summer and winter "projects" you can do yourself. Fresh paint, either on the inside or outside, is inexpensive and always a good method to improve appearances as long as the color selected is not too far removed from what most people find desirable. Other summer projects might include: cleaning up the backyard landscaping, removing a dead tree, or replacing a concrete driveway. A winter project could be replacing the baby blue ceramic tile and matching toilet in the master bathroom with a more contemporary looking ceramic tile and a water efficient toilet. Home Depot offers Saturday morning
courses on how to install the tile and you might find that you actually enjoy doing this sort of thing. Replacing older toilets with newer low water use ones will improve the looks of your home and you might get a rebate on your water bill.

I am reminded of how important the maintenance issue is regarding real estate every Tuesday and Thursday afternoon when I drive my youngest daughter to soccer practice. The neighborhood where the soccer field resides consists of homes that are between 35 to 40 years old. It is a nice neighborhood, but many of the homes do show their age. There is one home in particular that stands out from the others. It is a red brick home with white-painted wooden eaves. The roof appears to be the original. No "updating" or major changes seem to have been made to the exterior. The home, however, looks fantastic. The eaves are freshly painted. The front yard is nicely manicured. The trees and bushes have been trimmed and various flowering plants exist that give the home great "curb appeal." Every time I see it, I think to myself how much I would like to list that property if the owners ever decided to sell. Just by looking at the outside, it is "obvious" that the home has been well cared for and that the interior is probably in great condition. I am sure the property would sell fast and for a good price because of that first impression a buyer would get as they drive to the front of the property.

Home Buyer Worksheet and Checklist

Property Address: _____

List Price: _____ Monthly Payment: _____ HOA Dues: _____

Commute To Work (Miles/Minutes): _____ Taxes: _____

If you purchased this property, what would you change?

_____

_____

Neighborhood	Yes	No	N/A	Comments
Close to Schools				
Close to Shopping				
Close to Parks				
Neighborhood Problems:				
--Busy Street				
--Noise From Airplanes				
--Other				
Exterior				
Color				
Finish				
Roofing				

Garage			
Back yard			
Front yard			
Fencing			
Patio or Deck			
Sidewalk			
Driveway			
Pool			
Other Features			
Entry Way			
Walls			
Flooring			
Entrance Size			
Other Comments			
Family Room			
Walls			
Windows			
Lighting Fixtures			
Flooring			
Size			
Fireplace			
Other Comments			
Living Room			

Walls				
Windows				
Lighting Fixtures				
Flooring				
Size				
Other Comments				
Dining Room				
Walls				
Windows				
Lighting Fixtures				
Flooring				
Size				
Other Comments				
Kitchen				
Walls				
Windows				
Cupboards & Storage				
Lighting Fixtures				
Flooring				
Appliances Included				
Size				
Layout				

Other Comments				
Master Bedroom				
Walls				
Windows				
Lighting Fixtures				
Flooring				
Size				
Closets				
Other Comments				
2nd Bedroom				
Walls				
Windows				
Lighting Fixtures				
Flooring				
Size				
Closets				
Other Comments				
3rd Bedroom				
Walls				
Windows				

Lighting Fixtures				
Flooring				
Size				
Closets				
Other Comments				
4th Bedroom				
Walls				
Windows				
Lighting Fixtures				
Flooring				
Size				
Closets				
Master Bathroom				
Bath				
Shower				
Sink				
Toilet				
Size				
Other Comments				
2nd Bathroom				
Bath				

Shower				
Sink				
Toilet				
Size				
Other Comments				
3rd Bathroom				
Bath				
Shower				
Sink				
Toilet				
Size				
Other Comments				
Office				
Walls				
Flooring				
Lighting Fixtures				
Windows				
Size				
Other Comments				

Chapter 3: How to Select a Property to Use as an Investment/ Rental

Will this place make me money? Over the years, (the last two in particular) I have seen several examples of property purchased by investors turning out to be money losers. Most of the loses involved "flipping." What happened?

"Flipping" Homes

When real estate values are on the rise, **"flipping"** homes can be very profitable for investors. Flipping involves the acquisition of a home and then selling the home in the near future for a profit. There are two types of "flips:" the **"New Home Flip"** and the **"Fix and Flip."**

The "New Home Flip"

The **"New Home Flip,"** in my opinion, is the most interesting. When the demand for homes (especially new homes) is high and property values are increasing at a rate of 1% to 3% per month, many real estate investors will contract to build a new home for the purpose of selling the home once it is completed--this is a "New Home Flip." The process works like this:

> Assume an investor contracts to build a new home at the end of November with a planned completion date during May of the following year. If the home has a pre-construction purchase price of $300,000, a 2% appreciation (per month) would result in the home having a value, upon completion, of approximately $345,000. (Real estate agents are often the investors in this type of flipping because they are able to collect a commission, from the builder, when they purchase the home and only pay one commission, to the Buyer's Agent, when they sell it.) In this particular example, if the investor is able to sell the home when it is completed for $345,000, he/she could make as much as $40,000--even after a commission is paid to the buyer's agent. "Not bad" for just spending a few hours signing papers!

The really interesting aspects of "New Home Flipping" are the potential profits beyond the "standard" appreciation and the process of buying and selling the home. When the demand for homes is high, the supply of homes is low. In a "hot" real estate market, it is common to see home builders use "waiting lists" or even lotteries as a method to select buyers for their homes. (One home builder I worked with used the lottery system. Potential buyers had to attend the lottery drawing in person with an earnest money check of $5,000. Only five lots were "released" at a time and the "lucky winners" of the lottery had no choice as to which lot or model of home they could have--the lots and models of homes were assigned by the builder. If the potential buyers did not like what were assigned to them, alternate lottery winners would have the next opportunity to sign a purchase agreement. When the real estate market is "hot" it is amazing how many people will attend the lotteries and accept whatever the builder has to offer.)

As an investor, if you are able to get your name on the builder's list (or win the lottery to get the opportunity to build) you will find yourself in the position of being able to provide a product for sale immediately after construction is finished. This means that a potential buyer could get the home they want now and not have to wait. Moreover, buyers are usually willing to pay extra for the "privilege" of not waiting. For the investor, this might mean an extra 5%. In the case of the above example, this would mean an additional $17,245.

The closings associated with the purchase and sale of "New Home Flips" are also interesting in that they are sometimes "**concurrent**." This means that the investor buys the home from the builder at (basically) the same time he/she sells the home to the new buyer. This is the ideal situation in that it eliminates the "carrying charges" (i.e., mortgage interest, insurance, taxes, etc.) associated with owning and holding real estate.

If you should drive up to a new community and see real estate signs in the yards of newly constructed homes, this is probably a development that allows "flipping." Some builders will not allow "flipping" or will limit the amount of "flipping" in their communities. Builders often think that it "looks bad" to have "For Sale" signs in a new community and lenders become concerned when too many of homes in a community are sold to investors as opposed to actual residential buyers.

There are risks involved with "flipping" new construction. Even experienced real estate agents can not predict when the market will decline. I know of one investor, a real estate agent, who contracted to build a custom home with a builder that had a waiting list of clients. The investor had gotten his name on the builder's list early. When his name came up, the investor quickly contracted for the construction of a new home. The builder he used had systematic price increases built into the base price of their homes--every six months the base price went up 6%.The demand for homes was high. This looked like the perfect opportunity for the investor. Everything was going well--the investor even found potential buyers for the home while it was still under construction. The potential buyers wanted some upgrades to the home that totaled about $50,000. The investor agreed to add the upgrades during the construction. Unfortunately, when the home was completed, the "buyers" were no longer able to buy the home because of a job transfer.

About the same time the construction of the home was completed, the real estate market started to show signs of slowing. Homes were taking longer to sell and the investor, who was also a real estate agent, began to notice that there were not as many buyers looking for homes as there were just a few months earlier. The builder also noticed the decrease in sales activity--people on their waiting list began to notify them that they were no longer interested in building a home. The builder even had people cancel contracts on homes that were under construction and near completion. As a result, the builder had homes available for immediate sale and started to provide "incentives" (i.e., reduced interest rates for loans, $40,000 worth of free upgrades, free landscaping, etc.) to attract clients. The investor and the builder were now in completion! The investor became concerned and reduced the list price of the home he had built.

The investor was able to find replacement buyers--about four months after the home was completed. The replacement buyers had an agent that needed to be paid a commission. The carrying charges for the home, the commission paid to the buyer's agent, and the declining real estate market all worked to severely reduce the amount of profit made on this flip. The investor did make some money on this home (approximately $20,000) but in his opinion, it was not enough to justify the risk he took. When I talked to this person six months later, he informed me that he considered himself very fortunate to have sold the home. Real estate values had continued to decline and he believes that he could have lost as much as $50,000 had he not sold the home when he did.

The "Fix and Flip"

The **"Fix and Flip"** process is fairly straight forward. Investors locate a property in need of repairs/renovations, make the repairs/renovations, and then sell the property for a profit.

> The **"Fix and Flip"** system works because most home buyers either do not have enough cash to buy a property (and also pay for renovations) and/or the buyers do not want to live in a home going through renovation.

The obvious causes for failure with a "Fix and Flip" are investors underestimating the cost to repair/renovate the property and/or overestimating what the property would be worth after the modifications are made. Combine these two obvious causes for failure with declining real estate values and the likelihood of losing money is almost certain. What follows is an example of an unsuccessful "Fix and Flip:"

Case Study #2: "The Fix and Flop"

> An investor purchased an older home in a poorer part of town because it was much cheaper than other properties he had been looking at. He had "flipped" homes for several years and was skilled in many of the trades--he was able to do his own plumbing, electrical, and carpentry work. He knew the property required a lot of effort and capital to get it ready for sale, but he felt the low price he paid would result in a profitable outcome.
>
> He soon got to work replacing the roof, plumbing, wiring, and re-working the interior layout of the home to make it more appealing to today's buyers. After weeks of work and thousands of dollars of expenses, the major repairs and modifications were complete. All that was left was some minor cosmetic work including painting, new carpet, new doors and trim board, the installation of new fixtures and cabinets in the kitchen and two bathrooms, and some landscaping.
>
> One morning when the investor arrived to work on the property he found the back window of the home had been broken. Inside the home he found syringes, condoms, trash, and a piece of corrugated tin with a pile of ashes on it. During the night, people had broken into the house for shelter and had built a fire to keep warm. When he walked into one of the bedrooms he found even more problems--he found the people! He quickly called the police and soon the culprits were arrested and taken to jail. Instead of spending his work day installing new doors and trim board as planned, he

spent the day boarding up the broken window, cleaning up messes of human excrement and vomit, and sweeping up the trash he found on the floor. The two new toilets he had purchased, but not yet installed, had been shattered. Hundreds of dollars worth of power tools and hand tools he had stored in a bedroom closet were missing.

Work proceeded and soon the broken window was replaced, the interior had been painted, and much of the work on remodeling the bathrooms and kitchen was well underway. Some time later this investor arrived at his property to find yet another surprise. This time there were police cars parked in front of the house and the police had already arrested several individuals and were in the process of placing them into the back seat of their squad cars. As the investor walked to back of the home he noticed the same window had been broken out. This time, however, there was even more damage to the interior than before. He found more syringes, condoms, human excrement, and trash. (This was very discouraging due to the fact that the bathrooms were now functional!) He also found holes in the walls where someone had kicked in the dry wall and many of the new doors he had recently hung and painted had also been damaged.

He again cleaned up the mess and made repairs. More time went by and the home was near completion. Once again, however, he arrived at the property to discover that someone had broken into it. This time the back door was smashed. The people were gone and the interior had not suffered as much damage as it had during the two previous break-ins, but the newly installed carpet did need cleaning, many of the walls required touch-up painting, and the back door needed to be replaced.

The investor made the repairs, but instead of completing some of the landscaping projects he had planned, he called a real estate agent. The real estate agent did a market analysis and provided the investor with an estimate of what he thought the house was worth. The estimate was thousands of dollars less than what this investor had already spent on the home. The investor contacted other agents and their estimates were almost identical to the estimate provided by the first agent.

I do not know how much research this investor did concerning the neighborhood sales activity before he decided to purchase the property. I also do not know whether the investor underestimated the repairs, overestimated the potential profit, or how much the vandalism contributed to the loss he took on the property. I do know, however, that the property did go into foreclosure.

I found out about this property from an agent friend who was asked to list the property for sale by the mortgage company. When the agent checked the "comps" for sales information and summary data regarding the entire neighborhood, she found that there were very few sales in the neighborhood during the last two years. Of the three homes that did sell, all were foreclosures; including the subject property. The final sales prices for these homes ranged from $22,000 to $60,000.

The agent drove through the neighborhood and took notes concerning general neighborhood conditions. She was particularly surprised by the number of boarded-up and abandoned homes--there were five within just two blocks of the subject property and over a dozen within a one-mile radius. The overall condition of the neighborhood was very poor. The agent then visited the property she was listing to do an inspection. She found the inside of the property to be in very nice condition. When she went into the backyard she found a surprise--the investor who had lost the property to foreclosure. The investor seemed like a nice fellow; hard working and honest. He had coincidently stopped by the property for one last look. When he saw the woman with the clipboard walking through the house, he knew she was involved with the foreclosure and he felt the need to explain what had happened. He was the one who told the agent about the break-ins and the vandalism. The agent let the investor tell his story. She asked no questions. When the investor finished talking they said goodbye to one another and the agent locked the front door, placed a lock box on the door knob, and put her real estate sign in the front yard.

The listing agent, during her weekly inspections, found the property again broken into just a few days after she had talked with the investor. She hired a handyman to place plywood over the windows and board-up the back door to cut down on the break-ins. After four months, the property still had not sold even though it had been updated and priced thousands of dollars under the $60,000 that the investor had originally paid for it. Some time later, the mortgage company informed the agent that the property would be turned over to an auction company for disposal. The property sold at auction for $42,000.

I used the above case study to demonstrate to the reader that some properties might not be a good investment no matter how low the price. Remember, when the listing agent did her research on the property, she found that there were very few home sales in the neighborhood during the past two years. Of the three homes that did sell, all were foreclosures. Why didn't the owners of these properties sell the homes instead of letting them go into foreclosure? As the agent drove through the neighborhood, she also noticed five boarded-up and abandoned homes within two blocks of this property and over a dozen within a one-mile radius. Why were these homes vacant? Why weren't these homes sold or rented? If the homes needed repairs, why weren't the repairs made?

In my opinion, there were several "red flags" regarding the investment potential of this property. The information this investor needed to make a good investment decision did exist. It appears that he either failed to obtain that information or chose to ignore it.

<u>"Fix and Flips," require that the "fixed" properties be located in areas that will support the increase in value resulting from the modifications (i.e., repairs, renovations, additions) made by the investor.</u> Investors who do "Fix and Flips" should not expect to sell a $150,000 renovated home in a neighborhood where the highest sales price for the past two years is $60,000.

The "Fix and Rent"

Real estate values do not always go up, they can also go down. When the real estate market is "bad" (from a seller's standpoint) it can get very bad. **Foreclosures** and **Short-Sales** begin to appear as people find themselves owning property that has not only declined in value, but that value has declined to a level that is less than what they owe on the property. (See Chapter 2 for definitions and examples of Foreclosures and Short-Sales). How can investors make money in real estate during a declining market?

> *In a depressed real estate market that is "dominated" by foreclosures and short-sales, rents have a tendency to increase as property values decrease.*

This seeming contradiction is the basis behind the "Fix and Rent" method of real estate investing. As more property becomes available due to foreclosures and short sales, the cost of that property decreases. However, people still need a place to live. Since people who have lost a home to foreclosure (or sold a home as a short-sale) will not be able to purchase a home for a while, they are forced to rent. An increase in the number of people needing rental homes (i.e., higher demand) results in higher rents.

> *The combination of decreasing real estate values and increasing rents might provide profitable investment opportunities for many investors willing to purchase rental property. (Lower Property Values + Higher Rents = Potential Rental Properties)*

My local newspaper recently reported a story about an investor who had purchased nine single family homes over the last 18 months for a purchase price of less than $100,000 each. This individual then rents the homes for as much as $450 per month more than the mortgage, insurance, and taxes he pays on each property. Many of the renters are victims of foreclosure.

The above condition is not permanent. Investors need to view it as a brief "window of opportunity." Many factors will begin to interplay as rents go up. Eventually, increased rents will lead to an increase in apartment construction which will work to stabilize and even drive down rents.

I experienced this with three rental properties I owned near my former residence. I had purchased the properties seven years prior as part of my retirement portfolio. I deliberately selected properties close to my home so they would be convenient to show to potential renters and manage. The area where my properties were located has a major university and several high-tech companies located within just a few miles; it was a great place to have rental property. Unfortunately, some large investors found out about my little "Piece of Paradise" and decided to build hundreds of high-end apartment units across the highway from my rentals. These newly built apartment complexes provided fitness centers, club houses, and Friday night "get to know your single neighbors around the pool parties." As my leases expired, the amount of time needed to find replacement renters increased. I also had to reduce my rents to attract people away from the newer apartments with all the amenities.

The point I want to make to the reader regarding my above personal experience is that although rents might be going up now, rents will eventually stabilize and might even go down.

Investors using the "Fix and Rent" method of real estate investment must identify goals and develop an "Investment Strategy." Investors must understand that different real estate and rental markets exist and that these markets are constantly changing. It is impossible for me to provide my readers with an absolute solution or set of rules to follow that will lead to investments that will always be profitable. What I can do, however, is provide examples of what I have done.

The following is something I developed for myself (and my clients) to help identify potential investment properties. Although it might not apply in its present state to all potential investors, I think, with some slight modifications, my guidelines will help all people who are considering investing in rental property.

My Current Guidelines for Selecting Potential Rental Properties:

1) The property can be obtained for about 40% to 60% of it's highest historical value.

I like to check Public Records and the MLS to determine the Highest Historical Value (for the last ten years) of property I am interested in purchasing. If a property sold for $129,000 six years ago, I would consider a maximum purchase price at auction of $60,000 to be a possible good value under present conditions in my area. This will be subject to change and will need to be constantly monitored to reflect changes in variables like interest rates and potential rental income.

For example, assume the lowest priced property you can find for an investment can only be purchased for an amount equal to 80% of the highest historical value. If you are able to rent it out for more than the monthly costs associated with the mortgage payment, taxes, insurance, HOA fees, etc., you may still have a good investment. Not only are you looking at a possible 20% increase in the overall value of the property, the expenses relating to that property are being paid for by someone else, your renter.

Not all investments need to be "steals" they just need to be good investments.

It is important to note that I still check the MLS to determine the value of a property based on sold and active "Comps." However, unlike purchasing a residence, I am more concerned about the profit I will make on the property than finding a nice home for my family. Also, a residence is usually a long-term commitment. With an investment property, I am more inclined to look at the potential profit that can be realized by selling the property during the next market swing upward.

2) The property requires only minor repairs (i.e. carpet, paint, vinyl, etc.) and/or possibly a new furnace, water heater, and kitchen appliances.

The total cost of all repairs should not exceed ten to fifteen percent of the cost of the property. This is a personal preference of mine. I am not a "handyman" and with the exception of minor repairs, clean-up, and painting, everything else will need to be done by other people. I do not want to do major repairs or renovations and I do not like risking my money on large expenses.

Investors who are skilled in the trades do have the opportunity to make extra "sweat" equity. However, remember that it takes time and costs money to make repairs. Spending six months making repairs also results in six months of mortgage payments, insurance, taxes, HOA fees, etc., being paid out of your pocket and not by the renter.

3) The property is usually no more than 25 years old.

Older properties will require more repairs. Also, if you are considering the purchase of a condo, town home or any property with an HOA that is responsible for the exterior of the buildings, be aware of the HOA fees. As properties get older the HOA fees will increase to cover needed repairs. When the time comes to sell the property, high HOA fees will scare away potential buyers.

Investors buying older properties with HOA's that are responsible for maintenance items like the building exteriors, roofs, parking lots, garages, etc,. should also be aware of possible "special assessments." Special assessments correspond to large fees charged by the HOA to cover major repairs or renovations like new exterior siding, re-paving a parking lot, etc. The special assessments can be either "one-time" fees paid by the homeowners or extra fees added to the homeowner's regular HOA dues for a pre-determined period of time.

4) With 30% down, the property will rent in the beginning at a "break even point" or provide a positive cash flow.

The 30% down is a guideline I developed to help investors identify potential properties that might provide positive cash flow. It is based on current real estate values and rental markets in my immediate area. Different parts of the country and even different areas within my city may require less or more down to provide positive cash flow.

5) The property should be located within 15 minutes of your residence or work.

It is less of a headache to show or manage a property located close to your residence. The ideal situation is to have a property located close enough to your home so you can show it to potential renters after dinner or on weekends without taking up to much of your free time. If you are unable to locate investment properties close to your home, perhaps investment property located near your work is a possibility. This would allow the investor to be available before or after work for management duties.

Another option is to "cluster" your investment properties. If an investor is able to obtain two or more properties in the same area, this will at least allow multiple activities like showing one property and cleaning-up or making repairs to another during the same trip. I do not recommend having properties located all over a metro area. It is very frustrating and inefficient to spend time driving to and from properties scattered across town.

Hiring a property manager is also an option. However, this does take away from your profit. Property managers will usually take one month's rent as the commission for finding a renter and an additional 10% of each month's rent as the management fee.

6) I have no preference for town homes, condos, or single-family homes.

There are "pluses" and "minuses" associated with different types of residential rental property. For example, the HOA takes care of the exterior maintenance of a condo or town home and close neighbors will help prevent illegal activity like methamphetamine labs.

Single family homes with backyards are currently renting very well in my area. The reason for this seems to be people need a place for their dogs. Single family homes also have a tendency to appreciate better than a condo or townhouse. However, a single family home will usually cost more to purchase and requires more maintenance and upkeep expenses.

It has been my experience that condos and town homes have a tendency "to get hit first and hardest" by a down-turn in real estate values. As a result, condos and town homes are often more affordable for investors.

7) I currently have two general goals when selecting properties for investment.

The first goal is to find a property that should sell for at least twice the purchase price within the next 10 years. I use the **Highest Historical Value** to estimate the future value of the property.

The second goal is to have the rental income pay the mortgage payments and all other expenses (i.e., taxes, HOA fees, insurance, repairs, etc.) associated with the property.

The above are "guidelines" and sometimes I make exceptions based on how well I think the property will rent or if I think the property has a good chance of appreciating more than other properties currently available. To help investors determine the investment potential for specific properties, I have developed the following worksheet.

Worksheet:
Investment Potential
Sample Property 1

Property Address: 9020 --- Street

Description of Property: This is a 3 bedroom, 2 bath town home built during 1984. The property is located in a nice residential community surrounded by a larger subdivision of single family homes. The exterior of the buildings are in good condition. Six town homes in the complex have gone into foreclosure during the last 18 months and four other units are listed in the MLS as Short Sales. The final sales prices for these units range from $97,000 to $130,000

Repairs Needed: The property is in need of interior paint, carpet, a new stove, central A/C , and new blinds. The wood trim, baseboards, and interior doors are a dark mahogany and are scratched up and rough in appearance. I recommend they be painted a bright white to lighten up the unit and cover the scratches.

Potential Rent: It appears this unit will rent for about $950 per month. I talked to a neighbor next door and he is currently paying $750 per month rent. His unit is only a two bedroom and is dated in appearance. Results from checking the newspaper and Internet rental sites show monthly rates ranging from $700 to $1,000 for similar units in the area.

<u>**Highest Historical Value (HHV)**</u>: $179,900 (June 2002)

Based on 50% of HHV Max Bid: $ 90,000   Max + Premium: $94,500*

Based on 60% of HHV Max Bid: $108,000   Max + Premium: $113,400*

Based on 70% of HHV Max Bid: $126,000   Max + Premium: $132,300*

<u>**Loan Information Based on 30-Year Fixed-Rate-Loan at 9.5% with a Total Purchase Price of $94,500**</u>:

10% Down   Amount Financed: $85,050   Monthly Payment: **$715.15**

20% Down   Amount Financed: $75,600   Monthly Payment: **$635.69**

30% Down   Amount Financed: $66,150   Monthly Payment: **$556.23**

<u>**Monthly Expenses**</u>: Taxes: $153.00, Insurance: $17.00,** HOA Dues: $148.00

<u>**Probable Monthly Rent**</u>: $950.00

Net Monthly Income:

10% Down: $950.00 - **$715.15** - $153.00 - $17.00 - $148.00 = ($83.15)

20% Down: $950.00 - **$635.69** - $153.00 - $17.00 - $148.00 = ($ 3.69)

30% Down: $950.00 - **$556.23** - $153.00 - $17.00 - $148.00 = $75.77

Est. Costs of Repairs:		Money Needed at Closing:		Other Costs:	
Painting:	$4,000	Closing Costs:	$1,500	Rental Ad:	$ 800.00
Carpet:	$4,500	Loan Fee:	$ 850	Sign:	$ 10.00
Stove:	$ 700	10% Down	$9,450	Supplies:	$ 200.00
Central A/C	$2,000		--------		------------
Misc. Repairs	$1,000	**Total**:	$11,800	**Total**:	$1,010.00

Total:	$12,200				

Carrying Charges: Minimum of two months mortgage payments, HOA dues, insurance, utilities, etc.: $1,010 x 2 months equals $2,020.

Cash at Hand Needed to Purchase this Property: $12,200 (Repairs) + 11,800 (Closing Costs) + $1,010 (Other Costs) + $2,020 (Carrying Charges) for a total amount needed of **$27,030**

*Most auction companies are adding a 5% Buyers Premium to the final bid to cover costs associated with selling the property.

**Hazard insurance for the "shell" of this town home is included in the monthly HOA dues. However, with this property it is also necessary to get a landlord protection policy to cover the loss of personal property (i.e., carpet, cabinets, appliances, blinds, etc.) In other words, the HOA hazard insurance will cover the replacement of the structure from the interior drywall to the exterior of the building. The landlord protection policy will cover the replacement of material from the drywall to the inside of the unit including: interior paint, cabinets, fixtures, carpet, blinds, etc. Be sure to check with the HOA and your insurance agent with regard to the insurance package needed for an investment property.

The above work sheet (or one similar) is important not only in determining the maximum to bid on a potential property but also in the decision as to whether an investor can actually afford to buy a particular property as an investment.

Examination of the above information reveals that an investor would need to have approximately $27,000 on hand to obtain this property. This assumes the property can be acquired for $94,500 (maximum bid of $90,000 plus the 5% Buyer's Premium). With 10% down, the property would lose an estimated $83.15 each month when rented for $950.00 per month. It will not provide a positive cash flow until the down payment reaches 30%.

The above work sheet not only helps to document the costs associated with a particular property, but it will also allow investors to do "what if" scenarios. What if an investor could obtain the property for $85,000? What if the buyer gets a loan rate of 8.5%? What if the buyer does the painting himself instead of hiring it done.

As an agent, I like using the above work sheet as an educational tool to demonstrate to clients the actual cost of obtaining investment property. Investors are sometimes not aware that the interest rate for a loan on an investment property can be one to two percentage points higher than a conventional owner-occupied home loan and that they would need to put a minimum of 10% down. Investors might forget that they will be paying mortgage payments, HOA dues, insurance premiums, and tax payments while they are fixing-up and trying to rent the property (and other times when the property is vacant). Finding a property that needs fewer repairs and getting that property rented ASAP takes on a dollar value.

Worksheet:
Investment Potential
Sample Property 2

Property Address: 589 West --- Street, Unit A

Description of Property: This is a 1 bedroom, 1.5 bath town home built during 1992. The property is located in a town home community surrounded by three large apartment complexes. The exterior of the buildings are in good condition. The general area is near a major interstate highway so there is some traffic noise outside the units. Three town homes in the complex have gone into foreclosure during the last 18 months and one other unit is listed in the MLS as a Short Sale. The final sales prices for the above units as reported in the MLS range from $40,000 to $65,000

Repairs Needed: The property is in need of paint, carpet, vinyl flooring in the kitchen and both bathrooms, a new stove, refrigerator, dishwasher, and new blinds. The wood trim, baseboards, and interior doors are a dark mahogany and are scratched up and rough in appearance. I recommend they be painted a bright white to lighten up the unit and cover the scratches.

Potential Rent: It appears this unit will rent for about $750 per month. Checking the newspaper and Internet rental sites show monthly rates ranging from $600 to 850 for similar units in the area.

Highest Historical Value (HHV) for Subject Property: $125,000 (May 2001)

Based on 50% of HHV Max Bid: $ 62,500   Max + Premium: $ 65,625

Based on 60% of HHV Max Bid: $ 75,000   Max + Premium: $ 78,750

Based on 70% of HHV Max Bid: $ 87,500   Max + Premium: $ 91,875

Loan Information Based on 30-Year Fixed-Rate-Loan at 9.5% with a Total Purchase Price of $65,625:

10% Down   Amount Financed: $59,063   Monthly Payment: **$496.63**

20% Down   Amount Financed: $52,500   Monthly Payment: **$441.45**

30% Down   Amount Financed: $45,938   Monthly Payment: **$386.27**

Monthly Expenses: Taxes: $72.00, Insurance: $17.00**   HOA Dues: $165.00

Probable Monthly Rent: $850.00

Net Monthly Income:

10% Down: $850.00 - **$496.63** - $72.00 - $17.00 - $165.00 = $ 99.37

20% Down: $850.00 - **$441.45** - $72.00 - $17.00 - $165.00 = $154.55

30% Down: $850.00 - **$386.27** - $72.00 - $17.00 - $165.00 = $209.73

Est. Costs of Repairs:		**Money Needed at Closing:**		**Other Costs:**	
Painting:	$2,000	Closing Costs:	$1,500	Rental Ad:	$ 800.00
Flooring:	$2,800	Loan Fee:	$ 590	Sign:	$ 10.00
Stove:	$ 700	10% Down	$6,563	Supplies:	$ 200.00
Refrigerator	$ 850		--------		------------
Dish Washer:	$ 650	**Total:**	$8,653	**Total:**	$1,010.00
Misc. Repairs	$1,000				

Total:	$10,000				

Carrying Charges: Minimum of two months mortgage payments, HOA dues, insurance premiums, etc.: $750 x 2 months equals $1,500.

Cash at Hand Needed to Purchase this Property: $10,000 (Repairs) + $8,653 (Closing Costs) + $1,010 (Other Costs) + $1,500 (Carrying Charges) for a total amount needed of **$21,163**

Examination of the above information reveals that an investor would need to have approximately $21,000 on hand to obtain this property. This assumes the property can be acquired for $65,625 (maximum bid of $62,500 plus the 5% Buyer's Premium). With 10% down, the property would provide a net profit of $100.00 per month.

An investor considering the above two sample properties should study the differences. The smaller second property could probably be acquired for less out of pocket funds (i.e., $21,163 versus $27,300). The second property would provide a $100.00 per month positive cash flow with only 10% down as opposed to the 20% required by the larger town home to reach a near "break-even" point. If 30% is put down on the second property, an investor could have a positive cash flow of over $209.00 per month.

What if the buyer did not finance the second property, but paid cash instead?

> *The total amount needed to purchase the property would be $65,625 (maximum bid plus premium) + $10,000 (Repairs) + $1,500 (Closing Costs) + $1,010 (Other Costs) = $78,135.*

> *The total monthly income for this property would be $850.00 (Monthly Rent) - $72.00 (Taxes) - $17.00 (Insurance) - $165.00 (HOA dues) = $596.00. $596.00 X 12 months = $7,152 per year income.*

> *Dividing the yearly net income ($7,152) by the total amount invested ($78,135) will result in a yearly return of 9.1% on the $78,135 investment. (Wow! That does not even include the appreciation that might be realized when the investor sells the property!)*

Selecting Properties:

An investor who has identified **multiple properties** that fit into a predetermined investment strategy and **a maximum bid amount for each of those properties**, is now ready to attend an auction. All an investor needs now is to obtain one (or more) of the properties for the right price.

> *The exciting part about buying property at auction is that an investor will not know until after the bidding is complete if he or she is able to obtain any of the properties at an acceptable price. As a result, if one of the potential properties identified by an investor is currently being auctioned and it appears the property can be purchased for an amount equal to or less than a pre-determined maximum bid amount, my advice is to "go for it!"*

If an investor has planned on purchasing multiple properties and if other properties that meet the investor's criteria are available at the same auction, I recommend that the investor "go for them" as well. As I said during Chapter 2, "these properties will not last forever." There may not be other auctions.

If a property can be obtained for "much less" than it sold for during the last ten years and if it can provide a positive cash flow with an "acceptable amount" for a down payment, this is the time to buy. The "much less" for the purchase price and the "acceptable amount" for the down payment are the variables an investor must research and determine (for themselves) based on local real estate and rental markets and the investor's personal finances.

How Many Rental Properties Should You Have?

When determining how many investment/rental properties to acquire, investors need to consider both the effort and the risk involved with owning multiple properties.

Case Study #3: My Rental Properties

At one time my wife and I owned ten rental properties. (I wanted more, but there were no more available that fit my investment plan.) With the exception of one property, all of the units were just a few years old and in good condition. They did require painting and cleanup before they could rented, but no major repairs. Half of the rentals were located about 25 minutes from where we lived but were "clustered" together allowing us to work on multiple properties during one trip. The other half of the rentals were located closer to where we lived and also "clustered" near other properties owned by family and friends that were managed by my father-in-law. (My wife and I worked out an agreement with my father-in-law that gave him a 25% interest in the properties we owned in exchange for his management of the properties.)

My father-in-law was a real estate broker at the time and he was the one who found the properties for us. He did the research with regard to what similar properties were selling for at auction and provided us with an estimate of what he thought they would rent for. As I said earlier, the properties were fairly new and in good condition. Most important, we were able to buy the properties for about half of what they sold for just a few years earlier. These properties were FHA and VA foreclosures and only required 5% down to purchase. The Government provided the financing and we were able to get a positive cash flow with just the 5% down. (The positive cash flow only averaged around ten to twenty dollars per unit, but at least they did provide a positive contribution.)

Managing ten properties was a lot of work. I worked full-time at a "regular job" and the time involved managing the property would have made my life very difficult had it not been for the help of my father-in-law. As we purchased more properties, we needed to prepare them to be rented, show other properties to prospective renters, and make any needed repairs requested by our tenants. The agreement with my father-in-law also included my wife and I helping him prepare the units for renting on the weekends. During the first six months of owning investment property, most of our weekends and vacation time were used painting and cleaning our newly acquired rental properties. My wife and I were very fortunate to have Ed's assistance

The "risk" of owning rental property was always something I kept in mind while acquiring additional properties. My "regular job" as a contractor to the Department of the Army paid fairly well but could not be considered a "secure" position. I was originally hired for an 18-month contract. The contract grew and after 19 years I was still there. However, the 19 years consisted of several two- to three-year contracts with one 5-year contract. The possibility of budget cuts loomed and the environment was very "political." Every time I purchased a new property I thought to myself: "What would happen if I lost my job?"

All of the rentals provided a positive cash-flow. However, as I mentioned earlier, the amount of cash-flow ranged from only $10.00 to $20.00 per unit. If the units were rented, the rent I received covered the expenses, but what would happen if one or more of the units became vacant at the same time? The average purchase price for the units ranged from $35,000 to abut $45,000 per unit. With 5% down and an interest rate of about 7.5%, my monthly mortgage payments (including taxes and insurance) averaged just under $400.00--we rented the units for between $400 and $425 per month. If one or more of the units were vacant at the same time, or if one unit was vacant for a prolong period of time, it was obvious my savings would start to go down. What would happen if a furnace or water heater were to go out as well?

My wife and I are good when it comes to saving money. We pay our credit card balances in full at the end of each month and with the exception of real estate, we buy nothing on time. My wife and I worked for the same employer but she later left the company we were with for a better and more stable position with a large insurance company as a programmer. This provided us with a more secure financial situation. If there were layoffs at my job, I was the only one who could be out of work. Also, my wife and I had no children at the time--we were able to save our money.

As I look back, the ten properties were about all we could handle. We were fortunate that the rental market was good and that the properties were in good condition. Over the years the amount of money spent on repairs was minimal. The expenditures consisted of replacing two or three water heaters, carpet, and some paint. As time passed we sold some of the rentals and did 1031 Exchanges to acquire replacement properties located closer to where we live. I used the proceeds from the sale of some of the rentals to pay off the mortgages of the remaining rentals and to pay off the mortgage on our home. When we purchased replacement properties, we bought fewer and "nicer" properties in "better" neighborhoods. This resulted in more rental income from fewer rental properties. As of the writing of this book, I have only three rentals. My rentals are very nice, high-end town homes located within 15 minutes of my residence. My rentals are paid for and the monthly income they provide is a nice contribution to my semi-retirement. Yes, there are times I wish I had one or two more properties, but I am thankful for what I have.

Based on my personal experience, I recommend the following:

1) Acquire as many rental properties as you can afford.

Be aware that once you have over seven or eight properties, you must either devote yourself full-time to managing them or you will need to get help.

2) Own "Winners" not "Losers"

Winners provide positive cash flows and will not deplete your savings account or take up all of your free time because of repairs.

3) Be sure all of your investment properties have a good probability of yielding a profit when it is time to sell.

What was the highest value that this property (or similar ones) sold for during the last 10 years (i.e., the Highest Historical Value)? If a property sold for $160,000 five years ago when the real estate market was good (for sellers) there is a good probability that the property will again reach that value.

4) As the years go by (and as your properties increase in value) consider "cashing in" on some of them.

Use the proceeds to pay off the mortgages on the remaining properties (including your residence).

5) Get rid of the "Dogs!"

Instead of owning several properties, it might be best to sell some or all of the properties and replace them with fewer properties that are nicer, newer, and located closer to where you live. Quality is more important than Quantity. If you should find that some of your properties are difficult to rent or are beginning to require too many repairs, get rid of them! Ideally, the fewer replacement properties will provide the same amount of rental income--possibly more. (In Chapter 9: Selling Your Investment Property, I provide information on several "sell indicators" for investors.)

6) Work to increase your cash flow and to reduce your effort and risk.

Continue to be aware of the changing rental market and the real estate values in the areas you have invested in. <u>I do not recommend that you routinely raise your rents or constantly sell and purchase replacement properties</u>. However, if the rents in your area have increased significantly, it might be time to raise your rent. If, while researching real estate market values, you should come across one or more properties with a greater potential for profit (either from rent or long-term appreciation), it might be worth your while to sell an existing property and replace it with a "Super Winner."

Words of Caution:

There are many unknowns associated with investing. Jobs (both the investor's and the renter's) can be lost, rents can go down, unexpected repairs and major replacements (i.e., new furnace, water heater, roof, etc.) might be needed.

> ***Here I go again!*** *<u>An investment property that produces a positive cash flow is less likely to deplete an investor's savings. I recommend a positive cash flow.</u>*

If the worst should happen, the more an investment property contributes in a positive way, the less risk (and potential loss) experienced by the investor.

> *If the only way to achieve a positive cash flow is by putting more money down and obtaining fewer properties, then so be it!*

Chapter 4: Using a Real Estate Agent

The previous two chapters provided guidelines for the selection of investment property. In this chapter I will focus on why investors should use an agent to help locate and select the property.

Your real estate agent will play an important role in helping you determine relevant criteria and establish priorities for the selection of investment properties. The types of homes available, locations, and price ranges are just some of the criteria to be used in the selection of real estate. The number of homes on the market, summary sales information for similar properties in the same subdivision, concessions relating to those sales, etc. will be valuable in determining how much to bid.

> *Buyers will sometimes shop for real estate as if they were shopping for a car--they focus too much on the list price of a property.*

Buyers do this because final sales information on similar properties that have sold (for example final sales price and seller concessions) is not readily available to the general public. Haggling to get $10,000 off a list price of a home (or bidding $10,000 under the list price of comparable homes) might result in a purchase price that falls under the list price of many homes currently on the market, but this does not guarantee that the home was purchased at market value.

> *Important: In today's market, the list price on a home often reflects how much the owner owes on the property instead of what the property is worth.*

One of the most important services that a Realtor can provide to a client is a **Competitive Market Analysis (CMA).** (See Case Study #3.)

> *A **Competitive Market Analysis (CMA)** is a report created by a Realtor that compares the property that a client is interested in (i.e., the subject property) to other properties that are similar.*

The CMA will include information on the "Sold Comps" and an estimate of the value of the subject property based on those comps. I recommend that the CMA also include "Active Comps" (i.e., information on homes currently on the market). As I mentioned in Chapter 1, recent "Sold Comps" are usually the best indication of a property's market value; however, if the market is rapidly changing, "Active Comps" might be helpful in determining a future value. For example, if property values are declining, and if the list or "asking" prices for the "Active Comps" are less than the sold prices of the "Sold Comps", the "Active Comps" would be a better indication of the value of the subject property.

A detailed CMA will include information on the condition of the "Comps", sales **concessions**, and other information that can be used in the decision to buy a property and/or determining how much to pay for the subject property. Estimates of the costs of needed repairs, amount of rent that can be charged, and other "professional" opinions and recommendations should be included in the CMA.

> *Concessions correspond to agreements made between a buyer and a seller to resolve an issue that might have occurred during negotiations to purchase the home. For example, if it was determined that a home needed a new furnace, the seller might agree to provide the buyer with a $5,000 credit at closing in lieu of replacing the furnace. Other concessions might include the seller agreeing to pay some of the buyer's closing costs or the seller agreeing to pay "points" to "buy down" the buyer's interest rate. Since the concession amounts are not automatically deducted from the final sales price, the concessions need to be factored in to determine the actual value of a property.*

When buying a property, there is usually no cost to the buyer for the services provided by a real estate agent. The agent is paid a commission from the listing agent or the auction company selling the property. However, when using an agent to acquire an auction property, it is important that the written agreement between the buyer and the buyer's agent specify that the agent's compensation will be whatever the commission is that is being paid by the auction company. The co-op (i.e., commission to the buyer's agent) paid by an auction company is probably lower than what an agent would receive from a transaction based on homes listed in the local Multiple Listing System (MLS). Most auction companies will only pay a 1% to 2% commission to the Buyer's Agent.

Case Study #3: You Bid How Much?

Comparative Market Analysis (CMA)

Property Address: 2725 ---- Street, Unit 6   **Date: July 31, 2008**

Subject Property Details:

Style	Age	SqFt	Total Rms	Bed	Bath	Park	DOM	List Date	List Price
Condo	28yrs	1167	7	3	2	Off St	115	Apr 08	$68,000

Comments on condition, repairs, construction, location, landscaping, amenities, and other factors that would affect subject value:

Subject property is a bank foreclosure that is to be sent to auction. The building recently had new vinyl siding installed on the exterior. The interior condition is poor and the property is not habitable in it's present condition. The unit is in need of new carpet, vinyl flooring in the kitchen and bath rooms, and new interior paint throughout. There are no kitchen appliances. The manufacturers plate on the water heater reveals that it is less than 5 years old but the furnace and central A/C appear to be the originals. The bathrooms are in good shape but need a thorough cleaning and need to have caulking and vinyl flooring replaced. None of the bedroom closets have doors and trim board is missing in all 3 bedrooms. I estimate the repair costs, including carpet, vinyl, new kitchen cabinets and appliances, to be under $12,000. Five years ago 3 bedroom and 2 bathroom units in this development (in average condition) were selling for $119,000 to $129,000.

Describe the neighborhood and location (positive/negative features, safety, foreclosures, board-ups, distance to amenities, schools, shopping, transportation, churches.

Subject property is in nice location close to a major hospital, health clinics, and shopping. The complex is nearly 30 years old but has recently installed vinyl siding to the exterior of all buildings. The area is older and somewhat run-down. The two and three bedroom units in this complex sold well prior to 2003. The area has a good rental history.

<u>Active and Sold Comps:</u>

<u>Addresses:</u>

A1: 2720 West ---- Avenue, Unit -
A2: 2740 West ---- Avenue, Unit -
A3: 2725 --- Street, Unit -
A4: 2730 --- Street, Unit -

S1: 8678 ----- Street, Unit -
S2: 8675 ----- Street, Unit -
S3: 8657 ----- Street, Unit -
S4: 2710 West ---- Avenue, Unit -

Active	House Style	Age	SqFt	Total Rms	BD	BA	Prkng	DOM	List Date	List Price
A1	Condo	28yrs	1167	7	3	2	Off St	112	Apr 08	$ 92,000
A2	Condo	28yrs	1167	7	3	2	Off St	207	Jan 08	$110,000
A3	Condo	28yrs	1167	7	3	2	Off St	169	Feb 08	$112,000
A4	Condo	28yrs	1167	7	3	2	Off St	232	Dec 07	$115,000

Sold	House Style	Age	SqFt	Total Rms	Bed	Bath	Prkng	DOM	Sold Date	Sold Price
S1	Condo	28yrs	1167	7	3	2	Off St	566	Jun 08	$ 49,000
S2	Condo	28yrs	1167	7	3	2	Off St	23	Apr 08	$ 59,900
S3	Condo	28yrs	1167	7	3	2	Off St	4	May 08	$ 62,900
S4	Condo	28yrs	1167	7	3	2	Off St	11	Jul 08	$ 68,000

Comments on Comps:

A1 Not a short sale or foreclosure. All appliances included. Clean and nice condition.
A2 Average Condition.
A3 New carpet and paint, All appliances included.
A4 Property was purchased 4 years ago for $112,000.
S1 Bank Owned. Backs to greenbelt with view of mountains.
S2 Bank Owned.
S3 Corporate Owned.

S4 HUD Owned.

Subject Property Value Range:

As Is: $40,000 - $50,000   **Repaired:** $59,000 - $69,000

Other Comments and Recommendations:

Four other bank-owned and short-sale properties were reported sold in the MLS within the last 18 months but were not included in this CMA. Their final sales prices fall within the above range for sold homes. This would be a good property to bid on at auction. The needed repairs for this unit will probably cost under $12,000. Recommend maximum bid amount of $50,000 plus the 5% Buyers Premium. Unit should rent for $900 per month.

I prepared the above CMA for a property I wanted to purchase for use as a rental. The property was going to be sold at auction and I decided to attend the auction and see if I could buy it for an amount that would fit within my investment strategy. I went to the auction with my CMA in hand and a firm maximum bid of $50,000 (plus the buyer's premium) as my limit. The auction company's web site said the opening bid would be $1,000. I must admit the idea of obtaining a property for $1,000 was exciting. I knew the property would not go for a $1,000; however, it was possible that the property could be obtained for a very good price. I think everyone attending the auction was thinking "this just might be my lucky day."

When bidding on this property started, there appeared to be five or six people actively participating. The opening bid amount was $1,000. Several people lunged their bidder's cards forward to get the auctioneer's attention. The bidding went from $1,000 to $10,000, from $10,000 to $20,000 and within seconds the high bid was $60,000. The pace of the bidding slowed down and just two individuals were now being worked by the auction crew. One man held up his bidder's card to bid $62,500. A woman standing to the right of me then held up her card signifying that she would bid $65,000. The man reacted with a bid of $67,500. The woman to my right took a deep breath, stared at her friend and reluctantly held up her card to place a bid of $70,000. The auctioneer prodded the crowd for more bids-- there were none. The auctioneer then announced "We have our high bidder!" and the crowd applauded. The woman looked very happy. It had been a hard battle but she had won!

> *I looked at the winning bidder and I thought to myself: "You bid how much?"*

The $70,000 bid combined with the 5% buyer's premium resulted in a purchase price of $73,500. Examination of the above CMA reveals that eight similar units had sold over the last 18 months in this complex and their sales prices ranged from a low of $49,000 to a high of $68,000.

As I said earlier, I wanted this property as a rental. I had hoped today would have been my lucky day, but it was not. The pace of the bidding was so fast that I did not even bid. Since my limit was $50,000 it would have done no good for me to jump into the bidding action--my participation would only have added to the excitement and possibly driven the price up even higher.

The woman who was the highest bidder did not appear to have a realtor. (The person that was with her did not fill out any paperwork after the auction.) I wondered how this high bidder decided on the amount to bid? Did she collect brochures from the current listings in the complex or did she check on-line to see what the other properties were listed for? Since the current active listings were priced from $92,000 to $115,000 did she think she got a great deal because she only paid $70,000 plus a 5% buyer's premium? Would she be upset if she found out that she had just bid an amount higher than the highest amount paid in that complex for similar properties (but in better condition) during the last 18 months? Was the high bidder aware that this property was listed just prior to the auction for $68,000 in the local MLS? Did she know that real estate values in this area have declined over the last two years and that the decline seems to be continuing?

As a Realtor, I did have some other questions and concerns. When I was doing my research on the property I went to the auction company's web site. I checked the disclosure section. There was nothing unusual there. The web site had a link to Zillow that provided an estimate of the property's value. When I clicked on this link, information came up stating that the property had "recently sold for $62,000." No information concerning the details of this sale was provided. I then went to Public Records to check on the sale and nothing was reported. (This is not unusual in that it takes 6 to 9 months for sales information to be made available to the public.) If this property had, in fact, recently sold for $62,000, why was it now being auctioned?

I had other questions concerning this property and the high bidder. Was the high bidder going to pay cash for the property or did she intend to finance the purchase? Since the amount she bid was higher than the amounts paid for all the other three-bedroom, two-bath units that sold during the last 18 months (and since appraisers were "tightening" up their appraisals) would this property appraise for the amount she bid? Would a lender even consider financing a property that was not habitable in its present condition? Will the high bidder lose her earnest money? Will this deal fall through and will the place wind up back on the auction block in a few more months?

Perhaps this high bidder did know what the other properties had sold for and that the property she acquired was listed for $68,000 in the local MLS just prior to the auction. She might even have had a lender letter in her possession stating that this lender would finance the property to the amount she bid even though it was not habitable. It is possible that all these things happened--but I doubt it.

Did this high bidder make a bad deal? Possibly not. However, I do hope this person is not planning on moving any time soon. I am confident she will get back her initial investment and will make a profit if she stays in the home long enough. Based on my experience, I estimate that if she makes the repairs (that I recommend) she will be able to sell the property for over $110,000 in 8 to 12 years. Some of my Realtor friends think it will be more like 10 to 15 years.

A Realtor, who has done their job, will not only provide their client with information concerning the current market value of the property, but will also provide some experienced insight into possible difficulties with the transaction (i.e., getting a loan on a property that is not habitable) and additional information that is either not known by the general public or not readily available. Examples of this additional information might include: demand for rentals in the area and the range of rents being paid, new construction planned for the area, re-development being planned for a near-by retail center, past construction problems experienced by homeowners in specific developments, and proposed special assessments being discussed by the local governments or HOA boards.

Using a Realtor will not always guarantee that a buyer pays the lowest price possible for a property. There are too many unknowns. Just this morning the former director of the Federal Reserve predicted that the bottom of the housing market has yet to appear. He thinks property prices will continue to drop through 2009. Yesterday, one of the headlines on an Internet business home page stated that there is a new round of foreclosures just starting that resulted from people defaulting on stated income (i.e., "liar loans"). However, when a Realtor provides his or her client with historical sales information combined with professional opinions regarding the investment potential of particular properties, buyers will be able to make informed decisions using more information than is typically available to the general public.

Chapter 5: Financing Your Investment/Rental Property

This purpose of this chapter is not to discuss all the potential financing options available for real estate investing. Instead, I will focus on many of the issues that I believe investors should consider when selecting their financing. The major issue is how much cash the investor has on hand to use for real estate investing and costs associated with the investment properties. There are also many other issues that are important that will contribute to an investment being profitable or being a failure.

Traditional Financing:

It is necessary to inform people who are new to investing, that the minimum amount a lender will allow an investor to put down on an investment property is usually 10%. (In other words, the maximum amount that can be financed on an investment property is usually 90% of the purchase price.) It is also important to be aware that the interest rate for a 30-year fixed interest rate loan on an investment property will be about one to two percentage points higher than a loan for an owner occupant. Lenders do this because they believe a loan for an investment property is a higher risk than a loan for a residence.

I have, however, received information on investor loans that will provide money back at closing so that the investor will have money to put down on another property. In order for this to happen, the current property will need to be valued higher than what the investor paid for it. Even though this can be done, I do not recommend it. It is this type of potential overvaluing that caused the current real estate problems we are experiencing.

Alternative Forms of Financing:

Cash: An alternate to financing used by some investors is cash. Investors fortunate enough to have savings are always trying to locate safe investment options that will pay a return that beats inflation. Investing $50,000 in the purchase and repair of a small town home or condominium might provide an immediate return on your money that out performs CD's. It is a fairly simple task to total the expenses involved with the purchase, fix-up, and monthly maintenance of a property and then determine a percentage yield based on the net yearly income received on that property. An investor could end up with a 6% to 12% return on their investment.

Home Equity Lines of Credit and Refinancing Your Home: Home equity loans will allow investors to use the equity in their residence to obtain loans with interest rates lower than regular investment loans. A home equity line of credit will permit the investor to obtain money as needed to acquire the property and make necessary repairs. However, some limitations with home equity loans might exist with regard to the duration of the loan and possible future adjustments to the interest rate.

Refinancing a residence might be a better option. Investors who are able to refinance their home and pull money out to buy an investment property could find themselves in a situation where their current monthly payment stays the same (or is possibly reduced) but now they have a rental property completely paid for that is providing rental income that covers some and possibly all of their mortgage payment. However, keep in mind that the amount of the principal and the duration of their home loan has been increased.

Example of Refinancing a Residence to Purchase Rental Property:

A husband and wife have decided to purchase a rental property. They have located a three-bedroom, three-bath town home they hope to purchase for $90,000. The town home does need about $15,000 worth of repairs. The couple has over $30,000 in their savings account. They want to keep $15,000 in savings for future emergencies but are willing to use $15,000 to make the repairs to the rental property.

The couple wants to finance the purchase of the rental property by refinancing their current residence. This is a good option because of the following:

> 1) Interest rates for refinancing residences are lower than the rates on investment loans because lenders see the refinancing of residences as less risk than financing investment properties.
>
> 2) Interest rates have declined since the couple bought their home 15 years ago. The interest rate for their mortgage is 8.0%--current interest rates are under 5.0%.
>
> 3) The principle balance of their original home loan has been reduced because of the monthly payments they have made for the past 15 years.
>
> 4) Their home has increased in value since they bought it 15 years ago for $160,000.

The details of their existing loan are as follows:

> **$144,000.00**   Original loan amount.
>
> **$ 1,223.00**   Their current monthly mortgage payment PITI (Principle, Interest, Taxes, and Insurance) at 8.0% interest rate.
>
> **$110,500.00**   The approximate loan balance after 15 years.
>
> **$270,000.00**   Current market value of the home.
>
> **$159,500.00**   Current equity in home ($270,000 - $110,500 = $159,500)

The $90,000 purchase price for the rental property, combined with the remaining $110,500 loan balance, will result in $200,500 to be financed. The cost to refinance (i.e., loan origination fee, closing costs, etc.) will be approximately 2% of the loan amount (2% of $200,500 = $4,000) and will be added to the new loan. As a result, the new principle balance will be approximately $205,000.

Based on a 30-year, fixed-interest loan at 4.75%, the details of the new loan are as follows:

$205,000.00   New loan balance

$ **1,235.00**   The new monthly mortgage payment PITI (Principle, Interest, Taxes, and Insurance) at 4.75% interest rate.

$ **12.00**   <u>Increase</u> in monthly payment ($1,235.00 - $1,223.00 = $12.00)

Here is a summary of the **"Negatives"** and **"Positives"** resulting from the couple refinancing their residence to purchase a rental property:

<u>**Negatives:**</u>

- The couple now has 30 years remaining on their residential mortgage instead of 15.

- Their mortgage payment has increased by $12.00 per month.

<u>**Positives**</u>:

- The money received from the refinance will be used to purchase a rental property that they own "free and clear."

- There is no additional monthly mortgage payment for the rental property. In other words, since they did not get a separate loan to purchase the rental property, there will only one mortgage payment to make each month instead of two.

- The new mortgage payment will only be $12.00 per month higher than their previous mortgage payment.

- The monthly rent received from the rental property can be used to pay part of the mortgage payment on the residence.

- The couple received a lower interest rate by refinancing their residence as opposed to obtaining a separate investment loan for the rental property. A lower interest rate means they are making smaller payments and smaller payments result in more net profit from their rent.

Monthly Expenses for Rental Property:

$ 140.00   Property Taxes

$ 140.00   Monthly HOA Dues (Includes Hazard Insurance)

$ 10.00   Monthly Landlord Insurance Premium (insurance for personal property associated with the town home: cabinets, carpet, drapes, appliances, etc.)

--------------   --

$ 290.00   Total Monthly Expenses for Rental Property

Net Monthly Rental Income:

$1,200.00   Monthly Rent Received
$ 290.00   Monthly Expenses

-------------   ---

$ 910.00   Net Monthly Income from Rental Property

The rental property has the following monthly fees: HOA fees of $140.00, taxes of $140.00 and landlord insurance of $10.00. If we assume the property will rent for 1,200.00 per month, there will be a net rental income of $910.00.

What can be done with regard to the big "Negative" (i.e., the increase in the length of the loan) resulting from the refinancing?

When the couple refinanced their home to purchase the rental property, they only had 15 years remaining on their mortgage. The refinance extended the term of their loan to 30 years. Their new monthly mortgage payment is $1,235.00. What would happen if they not only paid their mortgage payment (as before but with a $12.00 increase) but also applied the $910.00 net rental income they received each month as an extra principle payment?

>*The extra $910.00 per month principle payment will result in their mortgage being paid off in just 11 years and 2 months. This is 3 years and 10 months earlier than their previous mortgage.*
>
>*Another option for this couple is to 1) pay their monthly mortgage payment (as before but with a $12.00 increase), 2) apply only a portion of the net rental income as an extra principle payment each month, and 3) use the remaining money for savings, investments, etc.**
>
>*There are many ways for the above couple to "view" the benefits of refinancing a home to acquire a rental property. My favorite is to "view" the purchase of this rental property as method to "pay their mortgage off 3 years and 10 months earlier that will also provide future, additional income." I suggest they apply all of the $910.00 net rent received per month as an*

extra principle payment.

*(Go to http://www.bankrate.com for a calculator that will help you examine how differing amounts of additional principle payments will reduce the length of a loan.)

Family/Friends Co-op: An option that might be of interest to some investors is a partnership or "co-op" agreement to purchase real estate. When my wife and I bought our investment property we formed a partnership with Ed, my father-in-law. Ed agreed to manage the property for us for either a fee of 10% of the monthly rent or a 25% ownership in the property. The 25% ownership option included an agreement to manage the property for up to six years (at no fee) in return for a 25% interest in the property. We chose the 25% ownership option and we agreed to help Ed get the places ready for renting by assisting with initial repairs and cleaning. We paid all expenses relating to maintenance and advertising and assisted with management activities (like changing out old refrigerators or managing the properties when Ed was ill or out of town). It should also be noted that Ed was the Buyer's Agent for the purchase of the real estate and did receive a commission from the seller when we initially purchased the properties.

At the end of six years we sold some of the properties but decided to keep most of them as rentals. Ed and I did market analyses on all the properties to determine their current total market value. We used this information to determine Ed's share of the rentals. Ed's share was roughly equivalent to the current market value of two properties. Ed decided that he wanted to own rental property instead of taking the cash, so I paid the mortgages off on two of the properties and then "Quit Claimed" them over to Ed. As a result, Ed's management services provided him with two rental properties that he now owned "free and clear." Ed continued to manage my remaining rentals for a fee of 10% of the rental income. I also continued to assist Ed with management activities for both his and my properties.

It is important to emphasize that property management can be time consuming and a lot of work. At one point my wife and I owned ten properties. We worked full-time in the data processing industry and it would have been very difficult for us to prepare the properties for rental, find renters, and perform routine management duties without Ed's help. If you are considering acquiring multiple properties you might find it necessary to have a property manager. A co-op agreement for the management might be an option to explore.

Some investors might have an interest is forming a financial partnership with family and/or close friends to purchase investment property. **If you do form this type of partnership, make sure everything is in writing**. Be sure to document how much each participant contributes financially, how expenses are to be paid, what is expected in terms of effort from each participant (e.g., initial fix-up, cleaning, property management, etc.) and include a predetermined estimate of how long the partnership will last. Remember, real estate investment is long-term; plan for at least a six to seven year time period. Finally, it is important to include an agreement on how the partnership will be dissolved if some of the members need to quit before the pre-determined time. Basically, partners will need to document, in advance, how the property is to be valued and how the remaining partners will "buy out" the individual(s) who choose to leave the partnership.

Minimizing Risk:

There are risks associated with real estate investing and I prefer to minimize those risks as much as possible. The information that follows is based on my personal experience.

In order to minimize risk, it is important to find investment properties that fit into a pre-determined investment strategy. As an investor, I want to know as many of the costs as possible associated with a particular property and the investment potential of that property. The associated costs include closing costs, costs to repair the property, and the carrying charges resulting from the time required to repair and find renters. The investment potential includes both short-term rental income and long-term appreciation (potential future sales price). In order to do this, I carefully research the condition of the property, the amount of money and effort required to get the property ready for renting, the probable rent I will be able to collect, and the expected sales price based on the Highest Historical Value.

The first thing you must do as an investor is to determine how much money you have to invest and from where will it come. As an investor, you will need to put money down to purchase the property and you will need to have money available for current repairs. You will also need to set money aside for future repairs and unforeseen problems. This can not be money you need for day to day living. Perhaps you have a CD coming due and you are not thrilled with the 4.0% the bank is offering you as an interest rate. Maybe there is a cash bonus you received from work or an inheritance you would like to invest in real estate. I do not want to see people investing their last cent in real estate or cashing out their IRA and putting all of the proceeds into rental property.

Side Issue #1: A Personal Note

> Prior to becoming a full-time real estate broker I was a project manager for a data processing company. The company I worked for had a contract with the Department of the Army to manage a large environmental data center. I left my position after 20 years and went into real estate full time. During my employment at the data center I contributed money to a 401k retirement plan and transferred the money to an IRA after I left.

> My 401k and IRA did fairly well. My account was with a large brokerage firm and my philosophy was to invest in low to moderate risk mutual funds. There were "ups" ad "downs" just like my broker had warned. As a whole, however, my retirement account did do well.

> During March, 2002 I had a bad surprise. The value of my retirement account got cut in half! My broker had assured me that my investments were in low to moderate risk, diversified mutual funds. How could this have happened? When I asked my broker this question, his only response was "None of us saw this coming."

> I was about to change my investment company and broker when I was informed that my previous broker had left the company. I talked to the person taking his place and he seemed like a decent fellow. He had a background as an accountant and had been a stockbroker for over 20 years. We met at my office and talked for about two hours. We talked about

investment philosophies, the problems I just experienced, and life in general. I liked the guy and decided to stay with the company. What the heck!

He made changes to my investment portfolio and things were going well. By February, 2008 my IRA had grown to an amount just 17% less than the high point I experienced during March of 2002. At the end of February, I noticed my IRA account value starting to drop again. By the end of August, 2008 my IRA had dropped in value to 26% less than it was on March, 2002. The US economy did not look good. Foreclosures were going up, unemployment was going up, the mortgage crisis hit Wall Street, and my IRA kept going down in value.

I was tempted to cash out my IRA and invest my money in a Self-Directed IRA consisting of rental property. I decided not to do this. I do believe in diversification. I must admit, however, that based on my personal experiences with real estate, I was confident that real estate would be a "safer" investment. After all, the price I would be paying for the rental property would probably be about half of what it had sold for just a few years earlier. Also, inflation will increase the cost of building materials and labor. Inflation does help real estate values.

Instead of cashing out my IRA and investing the money in real estate, I called my stockbroker and asked him to "park" my money into Government insured bank CD's for at least the next 18 months. I told him that I did want to go back into mutual funds when the economy got better, but for now, I wanted to keep my money safe.

He explained how placing my money in CD's would basically guarantee me a loss when inflation was factored into the actual return. I agreed with him but also reminded him of what happened to me during March, 2002. If I had placed my money in bank CD's then, "I would have a heck of a lot more money than I have now."

We also talked about the "ups and downs" of the stock market and how foolish it was to try to time investments. I did not argue with him. I do not like to see my money disappear. In the past I had experienced similar situations involving the stock market and did nothing. This time it was going to be different.

He agreed to put my IRA money into CD's and he took me up on a bet. I asked him to "pretend" I left my money in the mutual funds he recommended. I asked him to call me at the end of the next 6, 12, and 18 month periods and let me know how my IRA would have done if I had followed his advice. If, by the end of the 18 months, I would have made more money with the mutual funds he recommend, I would buy him lunch and say: "You were right." If, however, I was better off in the CD's, he would buy me lunch and listen to my thoughts about real estate investing. I do not know how this is going to work out.

Besides venting some of my frustrations about the stock market, I wanted to *share my temptation to dump my mutual funds and invest solely in real estate. However, I do listen to other people and I do value their advice to diversify. As a result, I will continue to invest my IRA in mutual funds--just not during the next 18 months.*

(As a post-script, six months has now passed. My broker called me yesterday and said I was "dead right." He asked me where I got my information. I told him that I read the newspaper. If I had left my money in the mutual funds he recommended, my account value would be less than half of what it is now.)

Once an investor has identified how much money he/she has to invest, an investor must then decide on how much money to put down on a potential property and how much to finance. My rule of thumb is to put down enough money so that the property will provide a **positive cash flow**. In some areas the amount required for a positive cash flow might be as little as 10%. In my area that amount currently ranges from 30% to 40%.

Investors with steady employment are sometimes tempted to purchase properties that will only provide a **negative cash flow**; in other words, the property will lose money every month. The investors might have a good income and when they factor in the tax benefits associated with rental property ownership, they feel comfortable that the monthly loss they experience will be off-set by tax benefits and the future (potential) increase in the value of the property. I understand the reasoning behind this decision but based on my experience and the experience of many clients and friends, I do not recommend it.

> **In order to reduce risk, I recommend that a property always have a positive cash flow.**

The amount of positive cash flow does not have to be much in the beginning, but it should be positive. In the future, repairs will need to be made to your property. There will be times when the property is vacant and money will need to be taken out of savings to make up for the shortage. It is assumed that rents will increase and so will your cash flow. If you experience years of rent increases, that is wonderful. However, this is not always the case. Rents can go down.

Chapter 6: Auction Day

Pre-Registration and Registration

All potential bidders will need to register on auction day immediately before the auction begins. Often, auction companies will allow people to pre-register on the internet (or by fax) prior to auction day. The information collected at this time is basic and consists of name, address, telephone numbers, e-mail address, etc. If you are planning to bid on a property, it is a time- saver to pre-register. Print out the registration form you completed on-line (or by fax) and bring it with you on auction day--you will need to confirm your registration.

If you are using a real estate agent, it is important that the agent also register in advance, usually by at least one business day. The agent will need to provide the name of his/her client at that time. The agent will also need to confirm his/her registration at the auction and attend the closing in order to receive any commission.

Some auctions have financing available at the auction site while others do not. See the specific auction details to determine the availability of on-site financing for the auction you are attending. If the auction company has an agreement with lenders to do financing, pre-qualification with one of those lenders is usually available at no cost or obligation immediately before the auction. This will be helpful in providing potential bidders (who have not previously talked to a lender) with an idea of how much they can afford to bid. Another benefit for using one of the lenders available at the auction site is that earnest money will usually be refunded if the buyer is unable to secure financing once they had been pre-approved by the on-site lender.

A sample purchase contract is usually available on the auction company's web site. Feel free to have your legal advisor review the contract prior to the sale. However, neither the auction company nor the seller will permit additions or changes to the form contract.

What To Bring

All bidders will be required to have a photo ID (i.e., drivers license), check book and sometimes a cashiers check payable to themselves in the amount of $2,500 to $5,000. If paying cash, proof of funds (i.e., copies of bank statements) might be required. Buyers who intend to purchase more than one property must have other checks (usually a higher amount) for each property they intend to purchase after the first.

Those buyers who plan to finance their property will need a pre-approval letter from their lender. Buyers who choose to finance through the lenders available at auction day will usually need to bring the last two years of tax returns, the last two years of W-2s, and the last thirty days of pay stubs.

Before the Bidding

If possible, have multiple properties in mind for purchase. Bring the property information with the pre-determined highest maximum bid recorded for each property. Buyers will not know the order in which the properties will be auctioned until the start of the auction. Sometimes the auctioneer will follow the order that properties are listed in a brochure, other times the order might be reversed or a completely new order is used. Buyers must be prepared to come early and stay late

Check the auction company's web site before you leave for the auction to make sure the property is still available. Some auction companies will allow on-line bidding prior to auction day. If a pre-determined amount is reached by the on-line auction, the property might be deemed "sold" and removed from the auction listing. If the property you wanted is no longer available, you still might want to attend the auction. It is possible, though not very likely, that the on-line high bid could fail and the property you wanted could wind up back on the auction listing. If this is your first real estate auction and the property you want is no longer available, it is still a good idea to go to the auction just to see what the auction is like.

Make sure you have fully previewed and inspected the properties you bid on and have reviewed the disclosures provided on the auction company's web-site or made available at the auction. There are usually at least two scheduled preview dates prior to the auction. If the property to be auctioned is listed with a real estate agent it might also be possible for your agent to arrange a private showing for you.

Many auction companies will provide a **practice auction** prior to the actual auction. The bidding at an auction is fast paced. The practice auction will give potential bidders an idea of how the process works and the pace of the sale. There will also be "bidding assistants" or "auctioneer assistants" who are there to assist with the bidding process and to answer any questions you might have.

Take Notes

Take notes during the auction. If the auctioneer uses a phrase you are not familiar with, write it down and ask your agent or one of the auction people what it means. Also, record the high bids for the other properties being auctioned. This could give you an indication of how much you will need to bid to get the property you want. If you are not the high bidder this time, the high bid information you recorded might be useful in determining the amount to bid at the next auction.

The Bidding Process

During registration, potential bidders will be given a bidders card. When the bidder decides to bid on a property he holds up the bidders card for the auctioneer to see. When the auction activity starts for a property you are interested in, I recommend that you do not be the first person to bid on the property. I recently attended an auction where an argument almost broke out between two people as to who bid first. It does not matter. It is not the first bid or the fastest bidder that gets the property.

During the bidding on a particular home, be aware of statements made by the auctioneer. Statements like: "People, know what you are doing before you buy this property" or "It has been brought to my attention that this property has problems" indicate that problems exist with the home that may not have been available when the disclosures were created.

The auctioneer may also make statements like: "This property is selling today!" or "The reserve amount for this property has been reached." An auction where the property is being sold with a "reserve" means that the property is being sold subject to seller approval. When a property is being sold "absolute" it will be sold to the highest bidder regardless of price. Any absolute properties will usually be noted in the brochure. Seller's will sometimes have representatives attending the auction who will be able to give the approval within minutes of the sale. Other times, however, high bidders will need to wait up to 10 days before they are notified of the decision to accept or reject their bid by the seller.

> **NOTE:** Except where prohibited by law, some auction companies may have their auctioneer start the bidding on any property by placing a bid on behalf of the seller. The auction company might even bid on behalf of the seller, up to the amount of the reserve price, by placing successive or consecutive bids on a property, or by placing bids in response to other bidders. If no bidders meet the reserve price, the seller is under no obligation to sell the property.

As the bidding continues, wait to see if the bidding slows down. If the slowdown occurs at a level less than the maximum amount you are prepared to bid, make your bid at that time. If the bidding is frantic and there is no slow-down, do not bother to bid. It will only help drive the price up. When you see people bidding higher than the amount you determine to be profitable for an investment property, you are probably bidding against someone who wants to purchase the property for their residence.

Many auction companies will have starting bids of $1,000 on select properties. This might indicate that the property has a problem, but usually the purpose of this low starting bid is to generate excitement and competition. Trust me. No one is going to be able to buy a $100,000 property for $1,000. Within seconds the high bid will be in the tens of thousands of dollars. (If not, and there is a lull in bidding, place your bid!)

> **Important:** Keep track of your bid. Auction companies will allow you to bid against yourself! If you are confused as to what the high bid is or who has made the bid, ask one of the auction attendants for assistance.

> **Remember**, a 5% buyers premium is usually added to the final bid amount. This buyer's premium is used to cover the costs of the auction and to pay the real estate agents involved with the transactions.

If you are the winning bidder, you will be asked to follow an attendant to an area removed from the auction site and asked to sign a winning bidder confirmation. The confirmation will show the winning bid amount, the amount of the buyer's premium, the total purchase price including the buyers premium, and other information on the specific property. This total purchase price does not include other amounts payable by the buyer at closing including closing fees, insurance, etc.

The winning bidder will then proceed to another area where the purchase agreement is signed and other documentation relating to the purchase and financing of the property is completed. (This is also the time when problems with the property might be disclosed to you. I attended an auction where 200 homes were sold and about 10 of them appeared back on the auction block within a few minutes after the winning bidder was announced.) This process will take between 30 to 60 minutes depending on whether or not you will be using one of the on-site lenders for financing. Remember, it is possible that the winning bid will not immediately be accepted by the seller and could be subject to confirmation. This is also the time when the high bidder is informed of how long it might take before they know if their bid is accepted.

The cashier's check (made payable to yourself) is signed over at this time. A personal check may also collected to make up any difference between the amount of the cashier's check and the amount needed to equal 5% of the purchase price on the first property and up to 15% of the purchase price for any purchase beyond the first. Some auction companies do not require the bidders to bring cashier's checks to the auction. Instead, they will allow you to use your personal check and then immediately deposit it electronically into the trust account of a title/escrow company. Make sure you have the funds available in your checking account before you bid at the auction.

The auction company will usually expect you to close within 30 days after the auction. Be prepared for delays. Do not count on the delays, but be prepared for them to happen. As a buyer, you will probably not be able to delay a closing. In some cases, the auctioneer and the seller may grant an extension of the closing date for the buyer. There is a fee for this extension and the fee is not credited towards the total purchase price. Typically, the auction companies and the sellers have the ability to extend the closing but the buyer does not. There are limits to the number of extensions allowed to the seller. More information can be found on the auctioneer's web site and within the Purchase Agreement that will be signed at auction. If you are financing your property, make sure your lender is aware that you are planning to purchase a property at auction and that the closing might be delayed.

On-line Bidding

Some auction companies are allowing potential buyers to make on-line offers on a property prior to the auction or during the actual auction event. Check the auction company's web site or brochures they provide to determine if all or some of the properties included in the auction listing are subject to early bidding and/or on-line bidding. If a property you want is subject to early bidding, I recommend you bid on-line. I recently attended an auction with a client to find that the property we were interested in had been sold on-line. I had checked the status of the property the night before the auction and it was still available. By the next morning, however, the property was gone.

Summary

The pace of the auction is fast and the atmosphere is exciting. When you attend an auction with the intent of purchasing a property, be prepared. A bidder should have thoroughly inspected the property prior to the auction and should have a firm maximum bid in mind. If you are buying investment properties, have multiple properties identified if possible. If a property meets your requirements and can be acquired for an amount at or less than your maximum bid, go for it!

Finally, expect delays with regard to closing. The buyer must be able to close within 30 days, but the seller has the opportunity to delay the closings. Stay in touch with the title company handing the closing. The title companies are often "slammed" with a few hundred closings at one time in an auction situation and the buyers who stay in constant communication with the title company are the ones who close earliest.

Chapter 7: Preparing Your Rental Property

Assuming you have acquired an investment property, now is the time to concentrate on the "middle part" of the investment cycle mentioned during the introduction of this book. This "middle part" (i.e. renting the property) allows the investor to hold the property until it is time to sell. Preparing your property to be a rental is "the beginning of the middle."

The Big Stuff

During the initial inspection of the property it is hoped that the investor did a thorough job of identifying the "Big Stuff" that needs to be replaced like the roof, furnace, water heater, carpet, appliances, etc.

If you buy a property that is 25 years old, expect to replace the water heater and the furnace. Look for rust at the bottom of the water heater and water leaking from the tank causing small puddles of water on the floor. If you see anything like this, have the water heater replaced immediately. Rust and/or water leaking at the bottom of the unit are indications that the unit is about to fail. When a water heater does fail, a very serious problem like a flooded basement could occur. If a furnace appears to be working, have it cleaned, serviced, and safety checked. It is not uncommon to find gas leaks, faulty valves, and ignition problems in older furnaces. It is much better to find the problem now than to have your renter call you late Saturday night, during the coldest part of the winter, saying that "the furnace went out."

Kitchen appliances are other big items. If your investment property is missing appliances, make sure the replacement appliances you purchase match the existing ones. A white refrigerator, tan stove, and a black dishwasher will not make a positive impression on potential renters. It might be worthwhile to remember that the color of the front panel on a dishwasher can often be changed by sliding the existing panel out and turning it over. This might save some money if you decide to buy matching appliances. If the appliances that exist in your property are "Avocado Green" or "Harvest Gold" get rid of them. They are at least 25 years old--buy new matching appliances. If you have a range hood, replace it with an over-the-stove microwave oven. It does not cost much more. People do not use regular ovens much any more except at Thanksgiving or to heat a pizza. An over-the-range microwave oven will be appreciated by your renter and will free up counter space in small kitchens. Also, do not make the mistake I made years ago when purchasing stoves for my rentals. I saved a few dollars by not buying self-cleaning ovens--do not do this. When buying a stove, buy one with a self-cleaning oven!

Painting the interior and exterior of a rental property are big items, but the relatively small cost of new paint provides big results with regard to the overall appearance of the property. When painting, keep the "Wow Factor" in mind. I recommend that the ceiling be painted a "ceiling white" and that the ceilings and the walls be painted with a "flat" luster paint except in the kitchen and bathrooms. Use a satin or semi-gloss finish for the kitchen and bathrooms. The reason I recommend a flat finish on the walls is that the flat paint will not show the seams in the dry wall and flaws in the finish like a semi-gloss paint. The flat finish will also have a softer over-all appearance because the light is not being reflected as much as it would be off a semi-gloss finish. Some people will recommend a semi-gloss paint because it wears better and is washable. There is truth to this, however, if there ever is a problem that requires the walls to be washed, washing walls will probably remove some of the paint and the walls will need to be touched-up anyway.

With regard to the paint color, the exterior of the home needs to stay in line with the rest of the community. You do not want you home to "stand out" from the others. If your home is included in a HOA, be sure to have the exterior paint color approved before painting. When painting the interior, I have seen many investors paint the entire inside, walls and ceilings, the same color, usually an "off-white." This is basically what the new home builders do and the home will have a clean and bright appearance. However, the interior will also look bleak and sterile. For only a few dollars more (even if you are hiring a professional painter) I recommend you paint the walls a color to contrast with the white ceiling. Yes, I recommend a "Realtor Beige" (i.e., medium beige) for the walls. When I show property with this color combination I always hear comments about how nice and fresh the home looks.

There are some exceptions to my "Realtor Beige" recommendation. If the rental property you purchased should have flooring in good condition and if that flooring is a green, gray or other non-earth tone color, it might be best to go with a matching wall color.

Many of the older properties will have dark woodwork: doors, trim, and baseboards. I recommend the woodwork be painted a bright white. The white woodwork will brighten up the interior of the home and the home will be more contemporary in appearance. There is another benefit to the white woodwork. It is common to find scratched trim and even a few hollow-core doors with "fist holes" in foreclosed property. These problems can be repaired with an acrylic filler and sandpaper. After the hole is filled and sanded, professional painters will apply an oil-based primer to the woodwork and then cover the primer with a semi-gloss bright white finish. The primer and the high-gloss white paint will hide the damage completely.

If you do decide to paint the baseboards, the carpet will need to be pulled back from the wall. It will be easier for the painter to just rip the carpet back and spray the baseboard. This will destroy the carpet. Therefore, painting the baseboards is something that I recommended investors consider when the carpet is going to be replaced.

Floor covering is the next big item to consider but one of the last items to complete. It might be necessary to replace toilets, cabinets, and possibly a few odd built-ins like a built-in kitchen booth or linen cabinet in a bathroom that looks dated and is in poor condition. These items will need to be removed and/or replaced prior to laying new flooring. I prefer vinyl flooring in the bathrooms, entry-way, and kitchen. It is relatively inexpensive and looks great. However, if you like to tile go ahead and tile these spaces. It looks great and will add to the value of the home when you sell it.

> **Water Conservation Rebates:** *If you do need to replace the toilets, check with the city or county in which the property resides to see if there is any type of rebate available for installing toilets with low water consumption. The city I reside in provides rebates for toilets and washing machines that consume less water.*

When carpeting, use a neutral color. Once again my choice is "Realtor Beige." Ask your real estate agent for recommendations for people to install carpet. Realtors often have sources for carpet and other services that can provide products for much less than can be obtained from local retail sources. The grade of carpet I recommend is referred to as "FHA Grade" and corresponds to the minimum requirements for homes financed by the FHA. Recently, a carpet vendor I use showed me an upgrade from the FHA Grade that only cost $350.00 more for a 1,200 square foot installation. It is a cut Berber that looks great. It definitely adds to the "Wow Factor."

An important point to make with regard to carpet is that there needs to be a balance between quality and cost. As an investor, you want the carpet to last and look good. However, it is going to be a rental for a while. Do not buy high-end carpet for an investment property unless you have a high-end property. Buy a good grade carpet that will last five to seven years. Plan on replacing the carpet at least once if you keep the home as a rental for more than ten years and again just prior to selling the property. Finally, stay with a neutral earth-tone color. Even renters will be turned-off to a bright green, red, or blue carpet.

The Smaller Stuff

Do replace torn screens, burned-out light bulbs, chipped sinks and chipped toilet seats. Remove the caulking from around the tub, shower, and toilet base and replace with new caulk. If your rental is a single family home, patch the dead spots in the lawn. Do other landscaping like replacing decorative gravel and wood chips. Plant new bushes and flowers. Pull weeds, apply fertilizer (weed and feed), and water (the heck out of) the lawn to get the grass to come back. Work on the lawn early so it has time to get in shape prior to renting it.

Clean, Clean, Clean

The next thing to do is to clean, clean, and clean. Make the place shine. Clean the windows inside and out. If the appliances are in decent condition and you are able to keep them, clean them on the inside and out. Buy new drip pans for the stove--they are available at The Home Depot and Lowes. Place boxes of baking soda inside the refrigerator to help eliminate any residual food odors. Buy a small bottle of Tang Orange flavored breakfast drink, poor it inside your dishwasher, and run the dishwasher through a complete cycle. The Tang will clean the interior of the dishwasher and help eliminate any interior stains and odors. Clean the light fixtures. Clean the toilets and the sinks. Clean the cabinets on the inside and out. Clean the outside of the furnace and the water heater! Potential renters will look at the place and say: "this place is really clean, even the furnace and water heater sparkle!" I have yet to have a potential renter (or homebuyer) say that they did not want a place because it was too clean.

The "Wow Factor"

As a landlord, you will know you have obtained the "Wow Factor" when a potential renter walks into your rental and says "Wow." Landlords should want to hear potential renters say "Wow" when they walk into the kitchen, bathrooms, bedrooms, living room, and the backyard.

The "Wow Factor" is not that hard to obtain. New paint, carpet, vinyl flooring, and appliances will take care of most of it. Two-tone designer paint (i.e., "Realtor Beige") on the walls with white ceilings, and white woodwork not only looks good but makes the place smell new. Small items like globe light-bulbs in the bathroom vanities and candle bulbs for the chandelier over the dining area are a big help. Replace any dim light bulbs with the highest wattage recommended for the light fixtures. This will brighten the home and will help transform a basement from a dark dungeon to an area with potential usage by a prospective tenant. If new appliances are needed, a new glass cook-top stove instead of a traditional burner stove might result in at least one "Wow" from potential renters. The glass cook-top stove only costs about $150.00 more. New towel racks, upgraded knobs and new handles for the kitchen and bathroom cabinets are fairly inexpensive. My father-in-law installed a new curved shower curtain rod in the bathroom of one of my rentals and that really brought out the "wows" from the people who were considering renting the unit. Not only does the curved shower curtain rod give the person in the shower more room, it also provides "a touch of elegance" to the master bathroom.

If a new kitchen faucet is needed, why not get one that allows the faucet head to be removed and used as a sprayer? My sister-in-law did this in her rental and when I showed the property to prospective tenants, I would walk to the kitchen sink, turn the water on, remove the faucet head and demonstrate the how the sprayer worked. The mother of one young man who was viewing the property was very impressed and told her son that she had been trying to get "Dad" to install one on their kitchen sink for two years. She added that she would be jealous! By the time they had finished touring the property, the young man definitely wanted to rent the town house. I took his application, but he was not selected by the owner. We had too many people interested in the property who were better prospects.

I am not proposing that investors go to extremes in giving the property the "Wow Factor." Unfortunately, however, investors sometimes scrimp too much and make a property look "cheap." Think in terms of allotting a budget for the "Wow Factor"-- perhaps just a few hundred dollars. When you are trying to attract potential renters, a few small things might make a big difference. Even in a good rental market where available homes for rent are going fast, an investor still should think of themselves as being in competition with other landlords to get the best tenants.

Case Study #4: The Woman With The Sparkling Clean Basement

Several years ago I was showing a buyer client of mine some homes when we came across one that really made an impression. The home was owned by a sales agent for a large home builder. This woman definitely understood the "Wow Factor." The home looked great as we drove up to the front of the house and when we entered the front door it was obvious that the home was owned by someone who understood how to prepare a home for sale. It was clean, it showed excellent, and it smelled good. Every room in the home looked liked it had been professionally staged. Yes, there were even freshly-baked chocolate chip cookies waiting for us in the kitchen. I had to ask the woman what she did for a living and I was not surprised when she told me that she worked as a new home sales agent for a builder.

I was surprised, however, when my buyer and I went down to the basement. The basement was sparkling clean. The homeowner followed us downstairs and said that she had scrubbed the basement walls and floor with a sponge mop and a mixture of hot water, detergent, and bleach. She had also cleaned the exterior of the furnace and water heater and washed the all the plumbing and heating ductwork. The basement windows were washed on the inside and outside, the window well casings were washed and the gravel lining the bottom of the window well had been vacuumed and perfectly leveled. Bizarre!

My client and I were stunned! We had never seen a basement, especially an unfinished one, that was so clean. The woman noticed the looks on our faces and said that it only took her a few hours to clean the basement and that she thought it was worth it. The basement not only looked good, but no longer smelled like a basement.

The impression this home left with my client and me was that it was well cared for and in perfect condition. It was also "obvious" that this home was worth more than similar homes in the same neighborhood. The comments made by my client after we left the home, however, were as surprising as the sparkling basement. Even though the basement in the home was unfinished, my client considered this basement as extra living space. He spoke about how his exercise equipment would fit perfectly in one corner and how his children could use the rest of the basement as an activity area. He went on to say that he thought his boys would love to "camp out" in the basement whenever he had company from out of town and this would allow the visiting adults to take their bedrooms. I am sure my client would not have considered having his children "camp out" in a damp-smelling, dusty, cob-web covered basement with spiders and bugs.

My client was interested in this home but since he had just started his search, he wanted to look at others. Within a few days the home with the sparkling basement was under contract. It was a quick sale. The lesson learned regarding the condition of this home also applies to rental property. People want to live in clean homes that are in great condition.

I must admit that I was not immediately sold on the benefits of a sparkling clean basement. Years later I had one of my rentals become vacant and the two women who eventually rented it asked if they could buy some paint for the basement walls and floor. My father-in-law, who manages my rentals, said "sure" and told them they could subtract the cost of the paint from the next month's rent. They mailed us the receipt for the paint and the reduced the amount of their rent payment accordingly. The paint cost less than $60.00 and it made my renters happy. What the heck!

After a year the two women had to leave due to job transfers. I went to check on the unit and get it ready to show to potential new renters. When I went down to the basement my first thought was "Wow." The painted basement looked great. Even though they had put up some shelves, it was obvious the two women had used the basement for more than storing Christmas decorations. They spent time in the basement and used it as actual living space. I remembered the home of the woman with the sparkling basement and decided to spend the next hour washing the furnace, water heater, plumbing, and ductwork.

I should also mention that just prior to the two women moving in, I had the unit painted and carpeted. I decided to paint the walls of the basement stairwell the same color as the rest of the house and I had planned on painting the stairs gray to match the basement floor. The stairs going down to the basement had looked very ruff. The person who had owned the property before me had large dogs and she evidently keep them in the basement at various times. The dogs nails scratched the wooden steps and the dogs also chewed on a few of the step edges. Due to the damage, I asked my carpet guy what it would cost to carpet the stairs. To my surprise it was only $150.00 more to include the stairs with the rest of the carpeting, so I decided to carpet the stairs. The painted stairway, the carpeted steps to the basement, and the painted basement floor and walls resulted in a great looking basement. When I showed the basement to potential renters they were impressed. Many of them also saw the basement as extra living space as opposed to just an unfinished basement.

The cost of a sparkling basement is just a few hours of labor. The benefits are many. If you have a few extra dollars, carpet the basement stairs when you carpet the rest of the home and paint the stairway when you paint the interior of the house. If you have a few extra hours, clean the basement. A basement that causes people to say "Wow" will help you get your property rented faster.

Properties that are in great condition do rent or sell faster. Also, renters will take better care of a property if the property is in good condition. I have had multiple occasions where tenants stayed in a property for one or two years and when they left, the unit was still in great condition and required no cleaning. We were able to place a "For Rent" sign in the window and an ad in the paper the following weekend. Since we did not have to spend time on cleaning, painting, and repairs, we were able to get the property rented faster and consequently, make more money.

Chapter 8: Renting and Re-Renting Your Property

I chose the above chapter title to emphasize that a relationship does exist between the past, present, and future rental activity of a property. As I mentioned in the previous chapter, a property that is rented in good condition often remains in good condition at the end of the lease. When a property is returned to the landlord in good condition, the landlord is able to get replacement tenants into the property faster and at less expense. Consequently, this chapter will focus on how to get your investment property rented initially and will also provide insight into how to reduce the amount of time, effort, and money required to find replacement tenants.

Get the Property Rented ASAP!

The old saying "Time is money and money is time," is especially true with regard to rental property. An investor is losing money every day the property is vacant.

In Chapter 3, I emphasized the need to select properties that require the least amount of effort and expense to get ready for renting. If the investor should find a property that does require extensive repairs, make sure the cost of obtaining that property not only includes the cost of repairs but also the carrying charges associated with the time needed to make the repairs.

Real estate investors must be aware that property usually does not rent (or sell) well during the winter months. This is especially true for the months of November, December, and January. Holiday activity and bad weather have a tendency to make people stay put. Also, people with children or people who are going to school, want to be settled into their home prior to the start of the school year. When deciding on a property to purchase as a rental, it is important to estimate when the property will be able to be rented. A property in fairly good condition with a tentative closing date at the end of July will have a good chance of being rented prior to the start of school. Another property with a similar closing date, but requiring three months of repairs and renovation, might not be ready until November. What happens if it takes you until March to find a renter? Make sure you have the ability to handle the expenses if the property is vacant for several months.

How Much Should The Rent Be?

Investors during the initial evaluation of rental properties should have determined a probable range of rental values. Call the rental properties in your immediate area to see what the landlords are asking for rent. Check you local newspaper and check various web-sites on the internet that feature rental property.

My father-in-law has a philosophy regarding how much rent to charge that I want to share with you. Look at the range of rents being paid and advertised for similar properties in your area. Make sure your property is in excellent condition and then base the amount of rent you charge on the middle rental rates instead of the higher rental rates. You will rent your property faster and will also increase the likelihood of retaining your renters.

When people do rent a place for an amount that is higher than average, it might indicate they had not shopped around enough or perhaps they were in a hurry to relocate. As a result, once they get settled, they will probably notice that their neighbors are paying less rent than they are and will look for a different place as they approach the end of their lease. So, even if a landlord does find someone willing to pay a higher rent, how long are they going to stay? One of the greatest expenses associated with rental property is finding new tenants. The total expense involved with a vacant property includes more than the costs associated with mortgage payments, taxes, insurance, and HOA dues. Cleaning expenses, repairs, advertising, and the time associated with each also need to be included.

When renting properties, landlords should remember that they are in competition with other landlords. Properties in excellent condition that are priced lower will rent faster. Also, remember the unknowns. Even in a good rental market, there is a limit to the number of renters available and the amount they are able to pay. If, after placing an ad, you receive very little response, do not be stubborn, reduce your rent!

Case Study #5: The Man With the Plywood Sign:

> *I still get amused when I think about a landlord in my old neighborhood who, for several years, had placed a large sign on the side of the road advertising a condominium he had for rent. The sign consisted of two large pieces of plywood joined together by hinges on one side. The sign would fold-out to make a "V" and on each side of the sign he hand-painted, in large letters, "2 Bedroom, 2 Bath Condominium For Rent." He included the price and his telephone number at the bottom of each side. He would place the sign on the side of the road starting Friday afternoon and leave it in place through Sunday night.*
>
> *Beside the general appearance of the sign, there were two other things I thought amusing. First, was the amount of rent he wanted. My family had two rentals in the same condominium complex. As a result, I was aware of how much rent was being charged for similar units. The man with the plywood sign always had his rents higher than all the other available rentals. The next thing that I thought amusing was how often the sign appeared on the side of the road. It seemed to be present for weeks at a time. If the sign did disappear for a while, it would re-appear again and again.*
>
> *The question I have is: **"Did this man ever consider how much money he lost by having the property vacant so much?"***

<u>Benefits of Long-Term Renters</u>

I recently lost a husband and wife as renters who had been renting the same town home from me for the past nine and one-half years. I bought the town home new and they moved in about two weeks after I closed on the purchase. Since the town home was new, it was in great condition. The rent we charged was in the middle range of rents being paid for similar properties. Our renters were wonderful. Their rent was always on time and they only called us when there was a problem. They treated the place like it was their own. During the nine plus years we only raised the rent twice. The increase in rent was a direct result of increases in the HOA dues and property taxes.

A few years ago, there was a problem with a large curved window in the master bedroom that resulted in water damage to the unit and required the tenants to stay in a different bedroom for over a week. My tenants were very cooperative and re-arranged their schedule to allow the workmen to make the repairs. Consequently, my father-in-law and I were able to have minimum involvement in the repairs of the unit. This saved us both a lot of time. When the repairs were finally completed, I thanked my tenants for all their efforts and told them not to pay the next month's rent. This was my way to make up for their inconvenience. They were very appreciative.

Finally, that dreaded day came--the day our perfect tenants gave notice that they were about leave. With housing prices in a decline, they rightfully decided that now was a good time to buy a place of their own. When they left the town home, it was in good condition. It did need new carpet, new vinyl flooring in the kitchen and bathrooms, new paint, and some minor repairs. Considering they had lived in the unit for over nine years, all of this was expected. We gave them back their entire security deposit and thanked them for taking such good care of the place.

The point I want to make with this example is as follows: I paid $131,000 for the property in 1998. By the time my tenants moved out during the summer of 2008, they had paid over $119,000 in total rent. They took care of the property, paid their rent on time, and only contacted my father-in-law when there was a problem that needed attention. It does not get any better than this.

How Much Should the Security/Damage Deposit Be?

There are two modes of thinking with regard to security deposits. Many landlords believe that requiring a new renter to pay the first and last month's rent in advance is the best way to ensure you get paid all your rent and have money in reserve to cover potential damage to the property.

My father-in-law has some different thoughts on this matter. Renters often do not have a lot of money. Coming up with two month's rent at once, while still possibly renting another place, might be difficult. Also, saying you require the first and last month's rent in advance implies that they do not have to pay rent for the last month. If a renter should decide to leave and just "go" without allowing the landlord to review the property condition with them, how are damages to the property going to be settled. As a landlord, you can always take them to court (if you can find them) but that is a lot of trouble.

My father-in-law recommends that you do not charge the first and last month's rent in advance. Instead, charge the first month's rent in advance plus a damage/security deposit. Prospective tenants are therefore informed that this portion of the money they put down on the property (i.e. the security deposit) has a different function. If the property is returned in the same condition as it was when they initially rented it, they will get their entire deposit back. If there is a problem, they will be given an explanation of the problem plus copies of any receipts to document the associated costs.

The Amount of The Security Deposit: *In terms of how much to charge for a security deposit, we recommend an amount between half and three-fourths of the monthly rental payment. This amount is noticeably less than a full month's rent but is large enough to cover part of the rent if the renter should "skip" and/or possibly the costs of any damage that might have occurred.*

Returning The Security Deposit: *As a rule, we try to give the entire amount of the damage/security deposit back to our tenants. Minor repairs, touchup painting, and carpet that needs to be cleaned are just part of what to expect with rentals. We do not charge our tenants for normal "wear and tear." It is just good business to stay on good terms with all your tenants, past and present.*

Several years ago, when I was single, I rented a small apartment that was in very nice condition. I took good care of it and when I left I expected to receive my entire damage deposit back. Instead, I received a refund check for $50.00 less than the full amount of the deposit--I was charged $50.00 to clean the oven. I had only used the oven once and that was to bake a pizza. I remember that a small piece of cheese had fallen off the pizza and landed on the bottom of the oven. The spot could have been easily removed by just scraping it with your thumbnail. (I had actually intended to do that, but I forgot during the move.) Since I was busy moving into a new home, I did not have the time to "fight this injustice" but I still remember it. To this day, if I ever hear anyone mention renting an apartment in that area, I will tell them about what happened to me and provide them with the name of the apartment complex as a warning.

Treat your tenants well and you will be rewarded. We have had tenants contact us years after renting our properties to inquire if we had rentals available in other areas. As an example, we had a man leave one of our rentals because he got married. Two years later, after getting divorced, he contacted us to see if the property he had previously rented was available. It just so happened that the property was vacant and he is again renting it.

Pets

Pets are a concern to landlords and should have an effect on what to charge for a damage/security deposit. A landlord should keep in mind that there are people who are allergic to pet hair/dander. Being able to advertise your property as never having pets could attract some renters. Unless the property you have for rent has a large fenced back yard, pets will probably spend most of their time inside the residence. Birds and fish are usually not a problem unless the tenants let the birds fly loose inside the unit. I have seen windowsills destroyed by droppings from birds using the same area as a perch. Ferrets are a problem in that their urine can leave a very pungent smell. Walls might need to be repainted and carpets cleaned and often replaced. Cats have a tendency to claw certain areas on a carpet, thus requiring repairs. A dog's toenails can scratch sliding glass doors and wooden floors. All of this assumes the animals are house-broken. If not, expect to buy new carpet.

However, having pets should not automatically be a "no" for landlords. Animals that are house-broken and well-trained can often be accommodated. For example, we currently have a town house rented to tenants with two Boxers as pets. The woman renting the town home is a professional dog trainer and the dogs are very well-trained and groomed. I have been in the property from time to time and it appears very clean and there are no pet odors.

The decision to allow pets might also depend on the condition of the carpet. If the carpet is over five years old and if it is starting to show some wear, you will need to replace it in the near future. I am more likely to allow pets when the carpet is getting close to the end of its life expectancy than to rent it to someone with pets when the carpet is new. If someone has a cat, the cost associated with repairing a small area of carpet damaged by clawing is relatively low, perhaps under a hundred dollars. (It is also a good idea to save a few pieces of carpet left over from the installation to make those repairs.) If pets are an issue, talk to the prospective renters about your concerns and possibly agree to increase the damage deposit by an amount that seems fair to both you.

Advertising

As soon as the property is ready to be rented, get the rental ad placed. It might be "OK" to get the ad placed a week or so early if the great majority of the repairs are made and only minor items like finishing some backyard landscaping or installing a new garage door opener remains. During the showings you can inform the potential renters of what you will complete prior to anyone moving into the property.

Do not show properties that still require a lot of work. Many people might be in need of a rental property immediately and showing them a property that is not currently available will be wasting their time as well as your own. Also, the site and smell of pet urine stains on the old carpet, filthy bathrooms, or the other disgusting things sometimes found in foreclosed homes, will not only make a bad first impression, but will also leave a somewhat permanent memory burned into the minds of potential renters. As an investor, you do not want people telling their friends who are also looking for a rental in the same area: "do not even bother looking at that place, it smells like a dog kennel!"

When it is time to advertise, I recommend you use as many resources as possible. A large "For Rent" sign (with your telephone number written on it) placed in the front yard or inside a front window is a good start. If the property has a Home Owners Association (HOA), be sure to check with the HOA as to any restrictions regarding the placement of signs. Usually, single family homes are allowed to have signs in the front yard. Condominiums and town homes often require the sign be placed inside a front window. Some condominium and town house communities will not allow signs of any type.

Placing an ad in the local newspaper is also recommended. Be forewarned that the ads are not cheap. I usually run my rental ads on Friday, Saturday, and Sunday. An ad like the sample I have below will cost about $450.00 to run during that time period. This is also a good time to have a real estate agent. The company I am associated with has an advertising contract with my local newspaper. I can run the same ad, because of the contract, for $150.00. If you are using a real estate agent, ask if they have a similar arrangement with your local paper. If so, ask the agent to run the ad for you and then reimburse him or her.

The are other low-cost or free advertising sources available. Craig's List is very popular and it is free. Some of my clients have used Craig's list and got excellent results. Keep in mind that you will probably need to resubmit the ad daily. Due to the number people advertising on Craig's list, your ad will continue to get pushed down the list. Various other rental property web-sites are available on the Internet. Usually, the local paper you advertise with will also provide an Internet web-site for people looking for rental property.

Church, school, and office bulletin boards can also be a good source for renters. If your property is located near a university or community college, the student housing office will often advertise your property on a their website or post a notice on a bulletin board. Word of mouth is very important. Tell your friends, neighbors, and relatives that you have a place to rent. Current tenants can also be a good source of future tenants. Ask your present tenants if they know someone who might be interested in renting the place. Perhaps they remember some friends who made comments during a visit about how nice the property was and how they would like to live in the area.

Below is a sample ad I have used in the past. Notice the abbreviations. Whenever I submit an ad to the newspaper, I ask my sales representative to review the ad and make any changes or abbreviations he thinks necessary and that can save money. He is usually able to shorten the ad by a few lines saving me between $15.00 to $30.00.

> TH, Villas at The Ranch
> (Federal & 120th) 2BD,
> 2BA, 1,230sf, Gas FP, A/C,
> att 1-car garage w/remote,
> enclosed patio. New
> appliances, paint, carpet,
> tile, sinks, and cabinets.
> Lndry Rm & W/D. Looks
> great! Quiet location.
> $1,050. Jack (my cell
> phone number)

Notice that I did include the general location of the rental in the ad, but I did not include the actual address. Have potential renters call you for the address. When prospective renters call, be able to describe the property in detail and have directions to the property available. If the caller wants to see the property, ask them for their name and telephone number so you can contact them if something should happen and you are going to be late to the showing or need to reschedule.

I hope you will be swamped with calls on the property. If this is the case, inform the callers as to the days and times you will have the property available to viewing. For example: "I will be showing the property this Saturday from 1:00 pm to 3:30 pm, will this work for you?" If not, ask them to recommend a time and day. If they say 2:00 pm to 2:30 pm on Sunday and if that works for you, get their name and number and let them know you will be there. When the next person calls you can now state that you will be available from 1:00 pm to 3:30 pm on Saturday and from 2:00 pm to 3:30 pm on Sunday. You do, of course, want to show the property to everyone who seems interested, however, it is nice to group the showings and not use up an entire weekend. Grouping the showings will save you time and might motivate a potential renter into making a decision when they see that other people are interested.

If you do not receive many calls, I recommend you do everything possible to accommodate people who do call. You only need one renter. If a person is having difficulty seeing rentals because of a difficult work schedule, the extra effort you make as a landlord to show the property might result in your acquiring a good renter.

Related Item Number 2:

My wife and I purchased a new ranch-style home during the summer of 2007. The purchase was contingent on the sale of our previous two-story home. The real estate market was slow. I had priced our previous home competitively, it showed great, and the home was in excellent condition. However, we were getting very few showings.

One evening I received a call directly from an agent who wanted to show my home to her clients at 9:00 that night. I have two young children and this was past the time we normally put them to bed. I asked the agent if we could instead have the showing a few hours earlier. The agent contacted her clients and called me back saying they would try to schedule a showing for the weekend. The weekend came and went but there was no showing. I called the agent on Monday and she informed me that her clients had decided to make an offer on a different property.

Several weeks later I received a call on my cell phone about 8:30 on a Friday night. I recognized the voice--it was the agent who had called me earlier with the late-night showing request. She asked if she could show my home to her clients that night at about 9:30. This time I said "of course!"

Just after 9:30 pm four cars pulled up to the front of my home. Two parked in my driveway and the other two parked on the street in front of my house. The group consisted of five or six adults, as many children, and a woman who appeared to be "Grandma." They took off their shoes, entered my home and proceeded to "take the place over." Some of them went upstairs, some downstairs, others were in the kitchen opening the drawers, checking the cabinets and the appliances, while others explored the backyard.

My wife, children, and I sat in the family room and watched the excitement. Things started to quiet down about 10:30. The adults then gathered around the dining room table to talk with their agent. About 11:00 pm I walked into the dining room and informed the agent that I really needed to get the kids to bed. The agent thanked me for the showing and within a few minutes my visitors were making their way out the door.

The agent called the next morning to inform me that she would be submitting an offer. After some negotiations, my wife and I accepted the offer. During my subsequent phone calls with the other agent, I was informed that the young couple who bought my home owned a small business and worked from 8:00 am to at least 9:00 pm everyday. I am glad I allowed that late-night showing--I only needed one buyer and "they were it."

Showing Your Rental Property

"Sell" your property as you show it. As you show your rental to prospective renters, be sure to point out the things that set your property apart from the others. New paint, carpet, central A/C, an electronic air filter on the furnace are important items to people allergic to pet dander. An upgraded kitchen faucet, a curved shower curtain rod, and new kitchen appliances are all things that can help you beat the competition. Outside storage facilities or garages with garage door openers and keypads might be overlooked by prospective renters--be sure to point them out. Information on bus stops, shopping, and nearby schools is also important to many people.

While showing your property to prospective renters, be sure to ask questions:

> *"How did you hear about this rental?" If everyone says they saw the sign or saw an ad in the paper, maybe you do not need to bother with entering an ad everyday on Craig's List. If everyone says they saw the ad in a small community paper, you may not have to bother placing an expensive ad in the large metropolitan paper.*

> *"Are you currently renting? Why are you leaving your other place?" If they say they are leaving the other place because their old landlord is a "jerk" or the neighbors are a "pain," ask more questions.*

> *"Do you have any pets?" As a landlord, you might not want a renter with two large dogs that thinks his current landlord and all of his neighbors are jerks.*

> *"Where do you work?" I am reluctant to rent to someone who is self-employed unless they can prove they have had the business for a while and can easily make the rent payments. I like my renters to have steady paychecks.*

> *"How long are you looking to rent?" Someone looking for a two to three year rental quickly moves up to the top of my list.*

Listen to what the people say voluntarily. If a young man says he has three motorcycles and likes to do his own repairs, how is that going to fit in with a rental property that has no garage? Is he planning on doing repair work on a tarp in the living room? It can happen.

Be Safe

Landlords do need to keep safety in mind when showing their rental property. After all, you do not know these people. There is safety in numbers, grouping your showings is one way to assure your safety. There are some precautions that everyone should take, not just women, when meeting people you know little about. For example, when leaving to show a property, let someone else know where you are going and how long the showing(s) should last. Bring a cell phone. If you must show the property late at night, bring someone with you. If your rental has a basement, let potential renters explore the basement by themselves, you do not need to accompany them. If someone tries to "lure" you into the basement to show you a problem, ask them to describe the problem and let them know you will take care of it at a later time. Assaults on landlords are rare, but they do happen. Trust your instincts. If something seems strange, stay close to the front door and say: "I have some other people coming in a few minutes, and I need to keep an eye out for them."

The Rental Application

A rental application serves two functions. First, it provides information needed to check on a prospective renter. Next, it contains information needed to contact the person if they should become a tenant.

When checking the rental applications of prospective renters, I make sure I have the following information:

1) Do they have a job? Does it pay enough?

2) What is the likelihood of continued employment? (Call the employer).

3) Why they are renting? How many people will be living in the rental?

4) Is there anything (i.e. debts or other financial obligations) that could interfere with their ability to pay the rent?

5) Are there pets? How many and what kind?

6) Have they ever been evicted?

7) Why are they moving?

8) How many vehicles do they have?

I do not bother obtaining credit reports on potential renters. They are not buying the place, just renting it. I recently noticed that some landlords in my area were charging a $60.00 application fee to prospective renters to cover the cost of a credit report and the time involved verifying application information. I think this will turn renters away. It does not take much time to confirm an applicant's employment status and to talk to a previous landlord.

It is not uncommon (or necessarily bad) to see that prospective renters do have (or have had) some financial problems. Some people find themselves in a position that requires three to five years "to get things back together." Perhaps they owned a failed business or were forced to make a major career change--they still need a place to live. As long as they have steady employment, they could be an excellent renter.

Selecting a Renter

The first thing I look at with regard to a potential renter is their employment situation. As I said earlier, I prefer not to have renters who are self-employed. I once rented a condo to a young woman who owned her own beauty salon. Her rent was late after the first month and when I talked to her about the problem, she informed me that her business was slow and that she had to make sure the rent and supply bills were paid for the business first. She explained to me that without the business income, she could not pay her rent. I explained to her that if she did not pay the rent when it was due, she would be evicted. The young woman made arrangements with her grandmother to provide her with short-term loans and her rent was on time for the remaining months of the lease. Thirty days before the lease expired, I informed her in writing, that she would not be allowed to renew the lease and that she needed to move.

As a result of other experiences like the above, I like to see renters who have jobs with regular paychecks. I call their employer to confirm employment and ask the employers to provide me with an opinion of the likelihood of continued employment for at least the next six months. I have had no trouble getting cooperation from the employers.

The next thing I look at is their reason for moving. People who are relocating from a different city to stay with a current employer or those who are moving to be closer to a new job are often good prospects. Divorce situations are also quite common reasons given on rental applications. Recently, I have seen an increasing number of potential renters citing foreclosure as their reason for moving. As long as they continue to have employment and the reason for the foreclosure seems legitimate, the applicants will probably be good renter prospects. (Examples of "legitimate" reasons for foreclosure include: an individual who is recently divorced and can no longer make a mortgage payment without the contribution of a spouse or a monthly mortgage payment that has increased to an amount the person can no longer afford because of an adjustable rate mortgage.)

Finally, a hodgepodge of other factors need to be considered. If, during a general discussion with a potential renter, it is determined that the individual plays drums in a rock band or did not get along with his previous neighbors, these are indications that you might not want to have them as tenants. As stated earlier, people with large dogs and those who enjoy repairing motorcycles might not be good choices if the property you have for rent can not accommodate the pets they have or the kind of activities potential renters plan to do while occupying the property. The most important thing I want to stress is the need for a landlord to ask questions of potential renters. If, as a landlord, you have concerns about a potential renter, ask questions. If you do not like the answers, keep looking for a renter.

Housing Discrimination

The federal Fair Housing Act and Fair Housing Amendments Act prohibit landlords from choosing tenants on the basis of:

- race
- religion
- ethnic background or national origin
- sex
- familial status, including having children or being pregnant (except in certain designated senior housing), or
- a mental or physical disability.

In addition, some state and local laws prohibit discrimination based on a person's marital status, age, or sexual orientation. Check with your local housing authority if you have questions.

One of the central objectives of the Fair Housing Act was to prohibit race discrimination in sales and rentals of housing. Nevertheless, more than 30 years later, race discrimination in housing continues to be a problem. The majority of the Justice Department's "pattern or practice cases" involve claims of race discrimination.

Sometimes, housing providers will try to disguise their discrimination by giving false information about the availability of housing, either saying that nothing was available or steering potential home renters or buyers to certain areas based on race. Individuals who receive such false information or misdirection may have no knowledge that they have been victims of discrimination. The Department of Justice has filed many cases against landlords alleging this kind of discrimination based on race or color. There are procedures that check for this type of activity on the part of landlords. "Testing" programs are in place in many communities that literally send trained people out determine if housing discrimination might be occurring.

Remember, landlords can select tenants using criteria that are based on valid business reasons, such as requiring a minimum income or positive references from previous landlords, as long as these standards are applied equally to all tenants.

Eviction

There will be times when a landlord is forced to remove (i.e., evict) a tenant from a rental property. An eviction might be necessary due to nonpayment of rent, violations of the lease agreement, and/or if the landlord has proof that the tenant or his/her guests committed violent and antisocial criminal acts. In the United States, the procedures for evictions are established by state law and do vary between states.

It is important for all landlords to understand that an eviction can only take place through formal legal proceedings. Locking a renter out of an apartment or house is illegal; it denies the tenant access to the property without due process. It is also illegal for a landlord to attempt to force a tenant off the property themselves by shutting off heat or utilities or by changing the locks. Tenants encountering such things may sue the landlord.

An eviction of a tenant must be done with a court order and that order is enforceable only by the sheriff or other officer of the court. As a landlord, if you should ever be in the position of having to evict a tenant, seek legal advice regarding your rights and responsibilities. Also, contact local law enforcement with regard to the eviction process and corresponding time periods.

Protect Your Assets

After you acquire your rental property, I recommend you talk with your attorney about holding each rental property in a limited liability company or other legal entity to protect the rest of your assets in case you are sued. Also, contact your insurance agent about adding an umbrella liability package to your homeowner's hazard insurance policy. You will want an amount that is at least equal to the total value of all your assets. Umbrella liability insurance is relatively inexpensive and will provide you with protection in case you are found liable during litigation.

Talk To Your Accountant

Tax deductions for depreciation and expenses such as repairs and mileage relating to managing your rentals can reduce your taxes and result in more profit from your rentals. Be sure to talk to your accountant to get a full understanding of all allowable deductions relating to owning real estate and rental property. Also, remember to save all of your receipts and record the mileage involved with managing your rentals!

Things To Make Your Life (As A Landlord) Much Easier

The following is a "Hodgepodge" of information that will save you time, money, and a lot of grief:

1. Winter Time: "Be Afraid, Be Very Afraid."

I think this is a quote from Star Trek--but I am not sure. The statement, however, does a great job of expressing my concern about owning rental property during the winter months. Here are some of my concerns:

> a) As I mentioned earlier, most property does not rent well during the winter months. Work hard to have the property ready for renting prior to September. The start of school and the winter holidays will put the damper on rental activity.

> b) If your property is vacant during the winter months, be sure to "winterize" the plumbing. This usually involves turning off the water and placing some sort of antifreeze in the toilets. Hire a company that does winterization to do this for you. They might have other recommendations specific to your location/climate that could save you some major repairs and expenses.

> c) Never turn the furnace off, set the thermostat to 60 degrees. I also

recommend that you keep the cabinet doors under the kitchen and bathroom sinks open to keep the pipes from freezing. (If you do have a potential renter who wants to look at the property, be sure to arrive early and set the thermostat to a comfortable level before they arrive so your prospective tenants are not cold during the showing. Close the cabinet doors during the showing and open them again after the people leave.)

d) If your property is vacant, check your property at least once per week-- even more if you are experiencing extremely cold temperatures. Remember, furnaces go out during the coldest days of the year.

e) Purchase two or three ceramic space heaters that your renters could use in the event their furnace goes out. When your renters contact you with the news that their place is "freezing" inform them that you will have a repairman there as soon as possible (probably the next day if you are lucky) and that you are on your way over with some portable space heaters. Your renters will appreciate your concern for their comfort and this will keep them from checking into a hotel and trying to get you to pay for it.

2. A small amount of time spent collecting information in the beginning can save you a lot of time and effort in the future.

a) Maintain a file containing the names of plumbers, electricians, garage door repairman, handymen, and HOA and HOA Management Company POC's and have that information readily available.

b) Maintain a file containing the contact information for your renters. Try to include cell phone numbers, work numbers and the name and telephone number of the nearest relative or friend you could contact in case of emergency.

c) Remember to have extra copies of all keys. You will have renters that lock themselves out, lose their keys, or it might be necessary to enter the property in case of emergency. If possible, be sure to contact your tenant before entering the property.

d) Record the brand name, make, model and serial number of all appliances, **especially the furnace and air conditioner**. When your tenant calls you at midnight saying that the furnace has gone out, you will be able to contact a serviceman and have the information they need to identify replacement parts.

3. Provide the name and telephone numbers of the various utility companies in the Additional Provisions section of the lease contract.

Remind your new tenants the day you give them the keys that they must contact the utility companies to change service to their names. I also suggest that you contact the utility companies to make sure the utilities are transferred on the day the renters take possession.

4. Buy smoke alarms and at least one carbon monoxide detector for each of your rentals.

If the alarms are battery operated, stop by your rentals yearly with replacement batteries and leave a note with your tenants reminding them to change the batteries. Hundreds of people are killed by fire and ventilation problems every year--you do not want anything like this to happen to your tenants.

Sample Rental Application

Jack Pantleo

xxx-xxx-xxxx Cell
xxx-xx-xxxx Fax
jpantleo@xxx.xxx **E-mail**

Please complete application with all pertinent details. If selected this application is to become a part of the lease agreement. A misstatement of facts in this application is justification for termination of tenancy.

_____
_____

How Did You Hear About This Rental?

Newspaper ___   Which Newspaper? _____   "For Rent" Sign ___   Craig's List ___
Other _____

Please Print

Last Name, First:_____

Birth Date:_____

Present Home
Address:_____

Phone #_____

E-mail Address: _____

Reason for Moving: _____

Spouse or
Co-Habitant's Name:_____

Present Rents:_____

Name & Ages of Children:
_____

Name & ages of occupants other than your children and applicant(s):

_____

Make and year
Of vehicles:

1st Car:_____ License #_____
2nd Car:_____ License# _____

Number and kind of
pets:_____

In case of emergency
notify:_____

Have you ever been evicted?_____ If yes, explain
_____

Present Landlord's
Name:_____ Address_____

Phone: _____
****

Applicants Employer:_____
Phone _____

Address:_____

Job Title_____ From _____ To _____

Gross Income: $_____

Applicant's
Previous Employer:_____

Phone _____

Previous Employer's
Address:_____

Job Title:_____ From_____ To_____

Previous Income: _____

Co-Habitant's Employer:_____
Phone _____

Address_____

Job Title_____ From_____ To_____

Gross Income: _____

Co-Habitants Previous Employer:

_____

****

Name of
Bank _____   Address _____

___ Checking ___ Savings

Phone Number: _____

Checking Account #_____   Savings Account #_____

Other Installment Payments:_____

Total Monthly Obligations: $_____

****

Name, Address, and Telephone Number of Nearest Relative Not Living With You:

_____

I (we) authorize any person or company to supply you with any information requested
concerning me (us).

Date_____   20___

Applicant_____

Co-Applicant_____

Notes:

Chapter 9: Selling Your Investment/Rental Property

When to Sell

There are several "sell indicators" that real estate investors should consider. The indicators include: reduction in rental profits, properties reaching their "maximum value," the tax advantages of depreciation coming to an end, "cashing in" to obtain a defined goal, and an investor no longer wanting to be a landlord.

Reduction in Rental Profits

The world changes. A property that was once a good rental might one day turn into a "dog." Earlier in the book I shared the problem I experienced with two of my rentals when a large apartment complex was built across the highway from my properties. My properties were very nice condominium units located in a quiet, up-scale community. The new apartment complex built across the highway included a huge pool, weight training area, and a large work-out room with the latest exercise equipment. Moreover, the apartment managers were hosting "Friday night get to know your single neighbors around the pool" parties. Soon after the complexes were completed, I noticed it took longer to rent my units. I was even forced to lower the rents to attract applicants. This was going on during the summer of 2005. Real estate values were still good (from a seller's perspective) so I made the decision to sell these units and replace them with one new rental property.

Real estate investors who want to take a more technical approach to the profitability of their rental properties, will examine the ratio of the rental income to the market value of the property. As that ratio becomes smaller, it might be more profitable to sell the current property and replace it with one or more properties in a different area.

The "Maximum Value" of the Property has been Achieved

I placed the words "maximum value" in quotation marks to emphasize that this is a judgment call on the part of the investor. I have two approaches I use to determine the "maximum value." I refer to the first approach as the Negative Factor Approach and the second as the Positive Factor Approach.

As the name implies, the **Negative Factor Approach** focuses on the negative aspects of a property. As a property gets older, more repairs are needed. If there is a Homeowners Association, the HOA dues might start to increase to a point that not only reduces the rental profit but could also scare off potential buyers. If the property is located within a part of town that is beginning to "show its age," that is also a problem. As the list of negative factors about a property begins to grow, so does my inclination to sell it.

The **Positive Factor Approach** focuses on the profit that can be made by selling the property. If a property is purchased in a area that one day becomes a "hot" market, it might be a good idea to sell the property and reinvest the profits into new developments that have the potential to be future hot markets. For example, assume that the property you purchased has more than doubled in value since the time you bought it. Why not sell the property and reinvest the proceeds into a new investment? Sometimes it does not seem possible, but "hot" markets do come to an end.

When searching for a replacement property, investors might want to consider new construction. New construction has many benefits. The obvious one is that it will provide a property in new condition--this means less maintenance for the landlord. Also, appreciation on new construction can be higher than what might result from older, pre-owned real estate. Builders often offer discounts on properties contracted to be built prior to construction of their models. This can result in some "instant" appreciation. There is another benefit to new construction--builders will often build systematic price increases into future construction phases. In a good market, this will provide some "systematic" future appreciation. Also, do not rule out buying the last property in a development. One of the town homes I purchased new was the last unit to sell. The builder was eager to close their sales office and I received a fairly good deal on the purchase.

The Tax Advantages of Depreciation Come to an End

Real estate investors are able to depreciate their real estate investments for 27.5 years. The depreciation corresponds to the improvements on the land and not the land itself. When determining taxes, the depreciation provides losses to modify the investor's rental income. This has a positive effect on how much money the investor is able to keep after paying taxes. Since the depreciation lasts for only 27.5 years, once the investment property reaches it's maximum depreciation, some of the tax benefits disappear. This might be a good time to find a replacement property.

"Cashing In" to Obtain a Defined Goal

The case study that follows is an example of a decision to sell property based on personal goals. The individual mentioned in the case study did not refer to charts of real estate trends to determine when to sell. He was not too concerned that he might have made more money by waiting to sell his property or by consulting with real estate experts. He knew what he wanted and he knew what it would cost. When the opportunity came to achieve those goals, he took it. **An investor should keep in mind that the ultimate reason for investing is to create wealth. The purpose of wealth is to acquire the things you want and need.** The man in the following case study accomplished both.

Case Study Number 6: The Diesel Mechanic at the Barber Shop

During the summer of 2006, I was in my local barber shop and overheard (and eventually joined in) a conversation between my barber and one of his customers. The customer was a 62 year-old man, formerly from San Diego, who was visiting his daughter in the north Denver metro area. He told us that he had just retired as a diesel mechanic after working 35 years with Caterpillar Tractor. Just three months prior to his retirement, he had made plans to continue working for Caterpillar for two to three more years. His goals were to save as much money as possible during that time and to increase the amount in his retirement account. He and his wife wanted to buy a retirement home in Arizona and spend some time traveling and visiting their children and grandchildren. The couple did their research--they knew the amount of money they would need to save during the next two to three years to purchase the things they wanted and to be secure in their retirement.

The man said that he and his wife owned an old home in San Diego fairly close to the beach. The couple had been keeping up with the property values in their neighborhood and they knew their home would provide them with a nice nest egg for retirement. One evening, they had a surprise. A young man knocked on the front door and introduced himself as a real estate agent. Before the homeowner had the chance to say "I'm not interested!" the realtor told him that he had a client interested in buying their home and that this person was willing to pay "a very large sum of money" for the property. (The agent actually told the homeowner the amount during that meeting, but the man did not want to share that information with everyone in the barber shop.) The man told us that he then called for his wife to come to the door and asked the realtor to repeat to her what he had just been told. After a few brief moments the man turned to the realtor and said "OK."

The retired diesel mechanic proceeded to tell us how his plans quickly changed. He retired from Caterpillar, bought a new Dodge pickup with a fifth-wheel trailer, purchased a retirement home in Arizona, and has spent the last month visiting his children and seeing the country.

After the retired diesel mechanic finished telling his story, I watched him drive off in the new white pickup truck. I still remember the look of excitement in that man's face and the tone of disbelief in his voice as he told the story of his recent retirement. I spent a few minutes thinking about what the man told us regarding the sale of his property, the things he had wanted (which he has now obtained) and his opportunity to retire 2 to 3 years earlier than planned. In my professional opinion, "He did good!"

When it comes time to sell your property, be mindful of your goals. As a Realtor, I often hear statements from my clients like: "I will sell my property when I can get $300,000 for it!" My question to them is: "What do you plan to do with the money?" If they tell me they have a goal of buying a new home, my response is: "If you can sell your property for $270,000 now and if that will allow you to buy the new home, would you sell?"

The value of real estate is (somewhat) relative. However, waiting to sell your property until some pre-determined and arbitrary price is obtained might include the risk of not being able to achieve your goal. In the example above, a $300,000 sales price would give the sellers "bragging rights" but it will not guarantee they will get "what they want, when they want it." Even if their property does reach the $300,000 mark in the future, the cost of the "goal" will probably go up as well. What will be gained by waiting? What will be lost?

The $300,000 example above corresponds to the amount that a past client of mine had as a goal for selling his home. During the peak of the last real estate cycle, my client could have sold his home (for $270,000) and purchased the ranch-style patio home on the golf course he wanted. He never did. This particular person is elderly and his main reason for wanting to sell his home was to purchase a ranch-style home with no stairs. Since the value of real estate is relative, he could probably still sell his current home and purchase a ranch-style home. However, there is one thing that should not be forgotten--he has climbed a lot of stars over the past five years!

As a final word on this matter, it is important to emphasize that even though the value of real estate can be relative, changes in value do not have to be the same across all properties. It is possible for one property to appreciate at a higher rate than another. If the new home on the golf course appreciated faster than the property to be sold, this client would have "lost" money by waiting. Investors must also be aware that real estate values can go down. Perhaps the value of the property to be sold has declined due to the construction of a large highway or some other undesirable situation. As an investor, do not forget the future "unknowns."

If you can get what you want or achieve your goal(s) by selling your property at an earlier time than originally planned---do it!

"Sick and Tired" of Being a Landlord

Being a landlord is not that difficult but there is more to it than collecting rents at the beginning of the month. Owning and managing real estate does require some sacrifice and there are frustrations. As a landlord, a person does need to have someone cover for them when they are out of town. A landlord should not expect to be able to take a 45-day world cruise when they own real estate unless they have someone they can trust to manage the property in their absence. Things do go wrong and they usually go wrong at the worst possible time.

When I talk to family and friends regarding what they do not like about being a landlord, it usually involves the time needed to clean/repair the property and the process involved in finding replacement tenants. (In other words, no one ever complains about collecting the rents unless the renter does not pay.) Much of the time and frustration involved with these issues can be reduced by having newer rental property located close to your residence. As I mentioned earlier in the book, it is really not much of an inconvenience to show someone a rental property when it only takes a few minutes of a person's time after dinner.

My personal plan is to keep my rental properties until I am in my mid to late sixties. This should correspond to the upswing in real estate values. However, I am not sure how I will re-invest the proceeds if I were to sell. Bank CD's do not pay much and since I already have my IRA in mutual funds, I do not want to put more money in the stock market.

My two daughters are eight and ten years old now. Perhaps I will just let them inherit the rentals…perhaps not. I do not know. If I ever get to the point of being "sick and tired" of being a landlord, that will probably be the time when I decide to sell my rentals.

THINGS TO CONSIDER:

Real Estate Values do Increase Over Time

Investors are constantly trying to identify clues, patterns, or other economic trends to help them predict the optimum time to buy or sell real estate. Basically, no one has perfected a model or theory that will accurately predict the "lows" or "highs" in real estate values, there are just too many uncertainties like wars and economic issues that come into play.

> *In my opinion, if an investor were to actually buy or sell real estate at the best possible time it would be the result of "dumb luck" and it would not even be known by the buyer/seller until at least two to three years after the purchase or sale of the property occurred.*

As investors, we do not know when real estate prices will drop to their lowest value or peak to their highest. We do know, however, when real estate values are "low" and we know when they are "high." Simply put, real estate prices have a tendency to be "low" when everyone is selling and "high" when everyone is buying.

With this being said, it should be emphasized that real estate values do increase over time. Inflation is often the primary reason for the increase. As the cost of labor and materials increases, so does the cost of building homes. If an investor was fortunate enough to acquire some property during times when the values had fallen to perhaps half of what the property might had sold for during the previous ten years, it is a good bet that the property will eventually return to that previous high value. This is probably a good time to sell.

Retirement Income

Rental homes are a good source of retirement income. People who do own rental property often find themselves in a situation where they do not want to lose the income they have been receiving. Moreover, when the investors compare the "return on their money" provided by their rental property versus what selling the property and investing the proceeds elsewhere would yield, many investors realize that they can not find a better investment.

Case Study #7: My Grandfather's Rental Homes

> *My grandfather was a retired medical doctor who owned two rental homes. The homes were located just a few blocks away from where he lived. I remember visiting him once when he asked my father to drive him to the rentals to collect the rents. I was seven years old at the time and decided to go along for the ride.*
>
> *When we arrived at the first property, my grandfather walked up to the front of the house and knocked on the door. The woman who answered the door greeted him with a "Hello Dr. Carter." The renter and my grandfather chatted for a while and then the renter handed my grandfather a small white envelope filled with cash. (My grandfather did not like checks.) My grandfather counted the money in front of the renter while the renter watched. After the amount was confirmed, my grandfather said "goodbye"*

and "I'll see you next month." We then drove to the next home and the procedure was repeated. The next stop was the bank. The entire process only took about 15 minutes.

The two rental properties were my grandfather's primary source of income during his retirement. I never once heard him talk about doing repairs or having any problems with his tenants. My grandfather was in his mid-eighties at that time and I am sure he just hired someone to make repairs on the properties whenever they were needed. With regard to problems with tenants, his two best friends were the Chief of Police and the County Judge. Perhaps that had something to do with why be never mentioned any problems with his tenants.

My grandfather's rentals were not sold until after his death. Not only did these properties provide retirement income for him, but they also helped provide income and retirement money for his children. When my grandfather died in the early 1960's, each one of his six children received an inheritance of about $15,000 cash resulting from the sale of the real estate. My parents owned a small farm and used the $15,000 they received to buy some ranchland so they could raise cattle as well as field crops they grew on the farm. The money they received raising cattle basically doubled their yearly income. After my father died, my mother sold the farm and the ranchland. She used the money resulting from the sale of the farm to buy a home in the Denver suburbs. When my mother sold the ranchland, she financed the sale of the property to some neighbors. The money she receives as a yearly payment on the sale of the ranchland provides her with retirement income.

A question that should be asked by all owners of rental property is: **"Why sell the property?"** Rental property provides an excellent source of income for retired people. Older people can manage the property as much (or as little) as they want and hire people to do the maintenance items they either can no longer do themselves or just do not want to do.

1031 Exchanges

Investors who find themselves "Sick and Tired" of being a landlord should examine the reasons why. If the reasons have to do with physical problems with the property itself, purchasing a replacement property could lessen or eliminate the problems they are experiencing. A 1031 exchange might be an option they want to consider.

A 1031 exchange allows investors to exchange the properties they own for other properties and defer paying federal and state capital gain taxes (up to 15% Federal, 25% depreciation recapture and applicable state taxes) if they purchase a "like-kind" property following the rules and regulations of the Internal Revenue Code.

For example, suppose an investor accumulates several rental properties over the years. Perhaps the rentals are requiring frequent repairs and/or are located some distance away from where the investor lives. A 1031 exchange can be used to reduce the management burden by allowing the investor to have fewer properties that generate the same (or possibly more) rental income, are in better condition, and are located closer to where the investor lives.

Closing Comments

In closing, my hope for any investor reading this book is that they will always make money with their real estate investments. I want them to make money from the beginning, in the form of a positive cash flow received from monthly rental income, and in the future, in the form of a large check they (or their heirs) will receive at a closing table.

> **Remember:** There are risks and headaches in real estate investing. However, properties that provide a positive cash flow reduce the investment risks and properties in good condition (located close to where the investor lives) reduce the headaches.

***